De-escalating
Children's Anger

DE-ESCALATING CHILDREN'S ANGER

USING THE **RESPECT** APPROACH TO
END THE POWER STRUGGLE AND
PROMOTE SELF-RESPONSIBILITY

JEFFREY SHOSTACK, PSY.D.

First printing, 2015

The information on *Nonviolent Communication* that is
presented in this guide reflects the author's understanding of
information from the following source:

Nonviolent Communication: A Language of Life, 2nd Ed.,
by Dr. Marshall B. Rosenberg, 2003, published by
PuddleDancer Press.
For more information, visit www.cnvc.org and
www.nonviolentcommunication.com.

This guide is not intended as a substitute for the advice or
support of a behavioral health professional. The reader should
consult a qualified behavioral health professional relating to
pediatric behavioral health matters and particularly with
respect to any symptoms that may require medical attention.

Library of Congress Control Number: 2014920999
CreateSpace Independent Pub. Platform,
North Charleston, SC

What others are saying:

Perceptive and inspiring, *De-escalating Children's Anger* brings necessary wisdom and universal insight to the challenges encountered with anger. In this important and essential booklet, Jeffrey encourages each of us to be mindful and responsible of our own understanding, participation and reactions of anger in order to effectively assist our children with theirs. He opens our hearts and minds to a deeper realization of the role we play and how we can bring about profound and lasting change in ourselves and our children.

Harold W. Becker, author and founder of The Love Foundation, Inc.

Dr. Shostack's book has been an invaluable resource to me both professionally and as a parent. His tools are practical and easily applied to real-life situations. It is an enjoyable read and will take the reader on a journey of self-discovery and personal growth. This book will help adults interact on a higher level with children. His tools will allow you to once again enjoy the parenting experience and be the parent you envisioned yourself to be!

Shirley Leibowitz, LCSW, psychotherapist

In this brief guide for adults who work with, and live with, a child who is angry and difficult to manage, Dr. Shostack provides a rich set of practical recommendations on how to defuse anger and how to build constructive relationships with the angry child. He does so in a non-blaming, accepting, and constructive way. And, he does so by invoking principles and practices that are evidence-based, not just arm-chair or "feel good" prescriptions. This is a guide that will be useful to many different adults, including parents, teachers, child care workers, mental health professionals and others. Given its brevity, it should not be a burden on the many adults for whom it is intended. It is highly recommended.

Thomas H. Ollendick, Ph.D.,
University Distinguished Professor
Director, Child Study Center
Virginia Tech

This is a well-written, easy-to-understand guide to dealing with children's anger issues. The examples were numerous, and the advice was concrete. It was impossible not to be helped by it.

Joanne Gurmankin, M.Ed., school psychologist

Contents

Acknowledgments

I owe a special thank you to Dr. Marshall Rosenberg, who developed *Nonviolent Communication* (*NVC*). This process has helped me, and numerous others, in improving our relationships. The ideas of *NVC* are essential to this book.

I would like to thank Dr. Thomas Ollendick, University Distinguished Professor and Director of the Child Study Center at Virginia Tech. Dr. Ollendick was kind enough to review my book and make suggestions. I believe his suggestions helped to raise the quality of my product.

Stephen Smith helped in the editing process and was of great support in our early discussions of publishing.

Thank you also to all others who reviewed my book, told me how it affected them, and made suggestions.

Part I

Introduction

I present an overview of what is to come in this guide and why I wrote it. I also describe a way that we can think about children's challenging actions. This way of thinking may be unfamiliar to many people.

1.

An Overview

The subject of how to interact with a child who is displaying anger elicits many strong and varying opinions. This situation can make it very confusing for someone searching for answers on how to respond to a child who is angry. What follows is a brief guide for adults who interact with frequently or intensely angry children, primarily ages five to twelve (although most strategies could apply to teenagers and younger children as well, sometimes requiring slight modifications). Such adults may be parents, extended family members, teachers, school administrators, childcare workers, or others. The basic steps are the same, regardless of the adult's specific role. The approach, while fairly simple to understand, is not always easy to implement. Trying something new, as the ideas in this book may be, can be very challenging. It is not easy for us to change our well-established ways. With this in mind, this guide is not intended to replace the needed services of a qualified behavioral health professional.

This guide is intended to be a very brief manual on what an adult can say and do to help a child who experiences frequent or intense moments of anger. I wanted to create a short but informative guide that I could recommend to parents, teachers, and interested people who may choose not to read a lengthier book. It is also important to me that readers can quickly learn the essence of an effective approach. Some readers will appreciate the simplicity of this type of guide. Other readers will understandably choose to go into more depth by consulting other works, including ones listed at the end of this guide.

Despite the short length of this guide, consistent and proficient use of the concepts presented here takes time and patience. For readers who are new to these concepts, this may require several readings and a good amount of practice in attempting to use the skills. In fact, I recommend reading one chapter and then contemplating the material and practicing the skills before reading the next chapter. After all chapters have been read, the reader can repeat the process as many times as needed until the material becomes sufficiently ingrained and the skills become automatic.

I would like to mention how I became interested in this topic. After getting my doctorate in clinical psychology, I worked in a variety of behavioral healthcare settings for children and adolescents. Such settings included children's residential treatment facilities, home-based and school-based behavioral healthcare settings, outpatient clinics, and private offices. From these experiences, I saw how children with even severe behavioral health diagnoses could work through anger and take self-responsibility when treated with respect and compassion. I also saw how interactions could become strained when children were treated otherwise.

I currently work as a psychologist in a large, urban, public school system. In this setting, I evaluate students who have a variety of learning and behavior issues. As part of my work, I frequently interact with students who are experiencing great frustration. I often ask these students questions to understand their issues. In our conversations, I have learned much about what these children think about, what motivates them, and how to help them to move in a productive direction.

From time to time, students come to me with a resistance to participating in the evaluation process. Occasionally, they even refuse. Rarely does the student continue along that path for more than a few minutes. Simple techniques that show care for, and interest in, their needs go a long way to changing the attitudes of these children.

In my work, I also speak with children who are in the midst of anger displays. Time after time, these children, who have no direct prior experience with me, come before me with angry expressions on their faces. A few minutes later, the same students are usually smiling and talking about constructive actions they will take.

I have seen schools with inadequate resources to care for children. The staff members are often under great stress. The parents at home are often under similar stress. In many places, the severity of the problems is great, and the problems have gone on for a very long time. There is often inadequate support for the people who have the responsibility of caring for these children. Such conditions can make it very challenging to take the approach that I describe. But it can be done.

I sometimes see children frustrated by adults who are demanding compliance, without showing attention to the children's feelings. But I believe there is a better way. My belief is that we can learn to effectively interact with children using a respectful dialogue, and often without using excessive power over them. Even when we must set limits and use adult power, we can do it in a kind way. Furthermore, in interacting with children in this way, we can feel much more satisfied.

This is a book on relating to the child who frequently gets angry and leaves adults feeling frustrated. I describe several key strategies that support the processing of emotions and prevent behavior problems that result from anger. These strategies involve establishing a relationship with the child in which the child is respected and helped to be understood. In addition, when appropriate, the child is given guidance in a patient and non-overbearing manner. These strategies can be disarming to children who are often used to engaging in battles with adults. But if adults refuse to engage in battle, then children may be willing to temporarily drop the challenging behavior. Then, the children become open to other interventions that will guide them toward cooperative, self-responsible behavior.

I would like to acknowledge Dr. Marshall B. Rosenberg, who created *Nonviolent Communication* (*NVC*). Dr. Rosenberg's work has been a great influence on my practice, and I use several of his concepts throughout this guide. For a list of local *NVC* organizations and *CNVC* Certified Trainers, please see www.CNVC.org and www.NonviolentCommunication.com.

I am not a certified trainer myself, but I have intensely studied *NVC* through attending classes, reading books, and attending ongoing practice groups over a several-year period. Any information on *NVC* in this guide is based on my understanding of *NVC*.

Using the RESPECT approach outlined in this guide, we will no longer need to rely on the use of guilt, shame, anger, and punishment to gain cooperation from these children. The emphasis will be on relating to children, rather than controlling them. Use of traditional power tactics will be discouraged when possible, because these tactics often lead to problems. When adult power over children must be used, I show how a compassionate attitude can limit the negative effects.

The steps in this guide are organized using three stages in the progression of anger: preventive actions the adult can take before the child is angry, actions that can be taken once the child is angry but before behavior has escalated, and actions that can be taken once behavior has escalated. At the end of the book, the process is summarized and examples of the process in action are given.

This book may trigger frustration for some people. It may especially frustrate those adults who have relied heavily on using force and punishment. It can be so tempting to use fear to motivate the child to behave in a certain way. Children can test our patience, and it can help us temporarily feel good to release our anger. Furthermore, some adults are very skilled in using their anger. I have seen some adults who, through the power of their voices, their demeanors, and their threats, were very effective in controlling children. But such children are learning through fear and are responding reflexively out of a desire to avoid punishment. And the motivating factor for desirable behavior is as important as the child's desirable behavior itself. After all, children who comply out of fear may return to their natural inclinations if they think they can get away with it.

If what you are doing is working for you, leading to satisfactory outcomes, and is not harming or abusing the child, then you may not be ready to change your approach; you may choose to continue your path. If you are unwilling to challenge your view that children must be punished to improve their behavior, then you may find this book to have little to offer to you at this time. But if you are frustrated by children who seem to resist your best efforts to scare them into submission or even reward them into compliance, then a new path might help get you to your destination.

Notes to the reader:
- Throughout this book, I attempt to use the plural in order to avoid use of gender-specific pronouns such as *he* and *she*. On occasion, this does not seem to read as well. In such cases, I sometimes alternate between male and female pronouns. In other cases, I write, "He or she...." Everything I present can be applied to both girls and boys.
- I sometimes use the expression "your child." In such cases, this expression can refer to any child for whom you are seeking support due to anger issues. "Your child" may include your son, daughter, or foster child. It may also include another family member, a student, or any other child. If you are a teacher, it may work well to keep a particular student in mind as you read.

2.

A Way to Understand Behavior

In his book *Nonviolent Communication: A Language of Life*, Marshall Rosenberg (2003) described a way of looking at behavior. With this approach, we can view everything people do as an attempt to meet a need. There are both physical needs and psychological needs. We have needs for belonging, respect, consideration, choice, and fun. But there are many needs beyond just these few.

So there is a positive intention behind even the most challenging behaviors of children. It is not always easy to identify that positive intention, but it is there. This perspective can make it easier to see children compassionately when they act on their anger or behave in ways that we do not like.

Common needs that children are trying to meet through their actions are fun, stimulation, respect, and autonomy (a fancy word for decision-making power about how to run one's life). Children who have considerable difficulties with anger generally use strategies that satisfy only some of their needs. Other needs of theirs are left unsatisfied. These faulty strategies often fail to satisfy their own needs for interpersonal connection, safety, learning, community, and peace (to name just a few). Even children with challenging behaviors have these needs. Therefore, we can view children who are acting upon their anger as doing the best they can to meet their underlying needs. Ross Greene (2014) described how the child with challenging behavior lacks important skills in areas such as frustration tolerance, problem-solving, and flexibility. Based on this idea, I believe that helping children to develop these skills would help them to meet their needs more effectively.

A more traditional behaviorist perspective suggests that the child's behavior is maintained by the events before and after the behavior. We can conclude that the consequences of a child's aggressive behavior may sometimes satisfy an important need of the child.

Skilled adults can use children's challenging actions to highlight (for children) the needs that are satisfied, as well as the needs that are not satisfied, by the actions. Then we can help children learn new strategies that effectively meet more of their needs.

Children experiencing anger may not comply with some of our demands. Children whose behavior we label as *defiant* are often experiencing a strong need for autonomy. In an attempt to experience decision-making capacity concerning their own lives, some of these children may even be acting out power struggles that they have witnessed or experienced. We can all relate to a need for being in charge of our lives. When someone tells us what to do, it can bring up (for any of us) a sense of discomfort at the idea of losing control of our own decisions.

Children who possessed strategies to simultaneously meet their needs for both autonomy and cooperation would probably not act in ways so frustrating to adults. But when children do not know how to simultaneously meet both of these needs, they sometimes act in ways that adults do not like. Adults may see this behavior as defiant.

Sometimes angry children use words toward us that we find offensive. Some people will say that such children are "disrespecting" us. What is the reason for this type of behavior? When children think negatively of themselves, they may want others to share in their unhappiness. This meets their need for companionship, as in the idea that "misery loves company." When children "disrespect" us, they may satisfy that need for companionship at the expense of their need for interpersonal harmony. Supportive adults can seek to understand the child's pain that prompted the statement. When such understanding is combined with other techniques, children may find new ways to get along with others while being okay with themselves.

Again, there are many needs. We need a sense of safety. We need affiliation with others. We need a certain amount of respect. The list goes on. If we view all behavior as an attempt to meet a need, then we can relate to all children (even when they are acting out of anger). By changing the way we view children, we can develop compassion for them. We can see children who behave out of anger as simply trying to meet their needs. We may not know just yet what that need is, but we are likely to eventually find out if we use certain tactics to be discussed later.

Instead of viewing children negatively, we can instead take ownership of our feelings. Children who act out of anger often trigger our own anger. It is better to take ownership of our feelings and admit we are angry than to speak of children as being "bad." Still, we can go even further in examining our feelings. Our anger suggests another underlying feeling such as sadness, fear, or hurt. Possibly we are angry at a child because we have a deep need for respect (or appreciation, or effectiveness), and we are sad when that need is not satisfied. By seeing the sadness behind the anger, we have taken yet another step in our connection to these children. Once we realize that an important need of ours is unmet, we can identify other means for getting the need met.

Children with high levels of anger have often given up on life to varying extents. One way we can see this is when a child frequently says, "I don't care." In residential treatment of the more severe cases, I sometimes witnessed children make that statement after staff members had threatened taking away privileges in response to negative behavior. And usually the children did lose privileges and continue to exist without a sense of remorse for the behavioral infractions. There is often a sense of hopelessness experienced by the child with severe anger. When the child is helped to regain a sense of hope, cooperation tends to increase.

Now we will proceed to the actions that can be taken by adults to help these children to begin new patterns of behavior that respect the needs of others while meeting their own needs. The word "help" itself may be somewhat distasteful, if we view the angry child as willfully malicious. Hopefully the earlier discussion about the dynamics of such children has given a different perspective. If we see children experiencing anger as needing help with learning more constructive ways to satisfy their underlying needs, then there are quite a few things we can do as we interact with them.

Part II

Before the Child Gets Angry

Prevention is usually easier than crisis intervention. When it comes to children who demonstrate frequent or intense displays of anger, we will benefit from preventing unneeded episodes of anger. Children will often be more teachable when they are calm. We can take advantage of this reality by teaching them critical skills while they are relaxed. They will be able to use the skills at a later time when their anger has been triggered. Similarly, we can teach ourselves important skills when we are calm and in an increased state of readiness for learning.

3.

Learn and Then Teach Self-Calming

Children who express their anger in less socially acceptable ways have a tendency to trigger our own emotions, especially anger. Once we are angry, our interactions with the child can get worse if we do not effectively manage our anger. Taking the time to engage in a self-calming activity can buy us the time to prevent our acting out of anger. Once we are calmer, we can deal with our anger more effectively. For those of us who interact with children experiencing strong or frequent displays of anger, it is important to master the skill of self-calming and to practice that skill regularly.

There are many ways we adults can calm ourselves. As we become skillful with self-calming, we will be better prepared for when our emotions are triggered. We can practice deep breathing. We can meditate. We can tense and then relax our muscles. We can talk to others to help us gain perspective.

It will not be easy for us to begin practicing calmness when we are very agitated. So it will be helpful to begin a regular practice of self-calming well before we are highly upset. This type of practice will help us to develop self-mastery. Next, we can begin to use the procedure when we are a little upset and eventually even very upset. This way, we will soon become skillful in achieving calmness when we most need to do so. The goal is to calm down quickly, so that we can respond rather than react when children are expressing their anger. Do you already have a self-calming ritual? If not, can you identify one to practice? Are you willing to practice it daily in order to master self-calming?

Once we are proficient in this skill, we can begin to teach it to children who need help with their emotions. By learning this valuable skill, they too will have an easier time using it when it is important.

For many children, the use of the calming breath is an effective way to reduce stress build-up. Several deep breaths, inhaling slowly and then exhaling slowly, can be a powerful relaxation procedure. We can practice this calming breath (or an alternative calming procedure) with children during calm times to get them used to the procedure. As they notice the pleasant sensations that arise from calming their emotions, they may enjoy practicing during random moments. Then we can begin to request that they use it when they are under mild stress as well. Eventually, after they have experienced the benefits of the calming technique in less stressful situations, we can encourage children to use the technique under more stressful situations.

For those who would like more detail on how to practice the calming breath during daily training, I will present one set of instructions that can be followed. (There are various sets of instructions on calm breathing.) The method I present is designed to be simple to remember and involves taking slow, controlled breaths from the diaphragm.

Inhale slowly through the nose for a slow count of four (or more, if you prefer). Pretend that you are blowing up a balloon in your belly, so your belly inflates as you inhale. Try to keep your chest still and relaxed. Only the belly should be moving. Pause briefly and then slowly exhale through the mouth for another count of four or more. Pretend that you are emptying the balloon of air, so the belly deflates. Wait briefly, and then repeat for a total of ten inhalations and ten exhalations.

When practiced during real-life situations, it may be necessary to reduce the number of calming breaths. Even one calming breath can be valuable, if that is all that time permits.

Children can also be taught additional anger management strategies before they are angry. They can be taught to use these additional strategies when they have gained adequate self-control but are still feeling very angry. Children can be taught to seek help from a trusted adult. An adult who listens with compassion is especially suited to provide relief. Children can be taught to take time away to regroup, going somewhere else to temporarily get their minds off the situation. Alternatively, they can be taught to engage in safe physical activity to discharge energy. Such physical activity can involve doing jumping jacks, running around, riding a bicycle, stretching, or even squeezing a lump of clay. Another strategy children can be taught is expressing feelings. They can write the feelings in a journal or a diary. Younger children can draw pictures of their feelings. Children can also express feelings by painting or coloring. By teaching these strategies to children well before intense anger develops, adults can make it easier to defuse this anger when it arises.

4.

Notice Your Feelings

A less commonly known but valuable tool for comforting ourselves when we are under stress is the process of self-empathy. Because of the power of self-empathy, I will present this aspect of the *Nonviolent Communication* process in some detail. Self-empathy involves connecting with how we feel and what we need. By engaging in this process, we can effectively move toward calmness. Self-empathy is a seemingly simple process, but it takes time and practice to get proficient at it. And empathy for oneself is critical for doing the upcoming work with the child. So how do we do this?

We begin the process of self-empathy by noticing the feelings within us. All people experience feelings, but we do not always pay much attention to these feelings. In fact, we are often taught to get over our feelings.

Why bother getting in touch with our feelings at all? For starters, feelings give us useful information about what we need and do not need. A very basic example is feeling tired, which suggests a need for rest. When we have unpleasant feelings, it means that a need is not being met. When we have pleasant feelings, a need is being met.

Suppose a child does not follow our instruction to come inside before it is dark outside. Because our feelings are related to our thoughts and our needs, there are various possibilities as to what we may feel in such a situation. Suppose a feeling of fear is triggered within us when the child does not follow the instruction. This fear may be telling us that safety is important to us.

Other children may trigger a feeling of sadness within us when they call another child a name intended to insult that child. This sadness may inform us that consideration and respect are important to us.

Another child who does not respond when we attempt to resolve an issue may trigger our sadness. This sadness might signal us that we have a wish for interpersonal connection.

And yet another child who tells us to "shut up" may trigger our anger. Anger is a different kind of feeling than sadness, fear, or frustration. Anger implies that we made a judgment about someone for that person's behavior. It is helpful in the case of anger to recognize the judgment and to loosen our attachment to it. We can usually find another core feeling, often sadness, fear, or frustration. Then we can once again identify what we need, whether it is respect, consideration, or some other need.

When we have needs that are unfulfilled, we may feel (for example) sad, frustrated, afraid, annoyed, or angry. When our needs are met, we may feel (for example) happy, joyous, relaxed, content, calm, interested, or comfortable.

We sometimes say things like, "I feel that Jim wants to get out of working." Or, "I feel like I need a break." These are not true feelings, but rather thoughts. When the word "that" or "like" follows the "feel" in a sentence, it is likely that a thought rather than a feeling is being expressed.

There are some words that can follow the word "feel" and sound like feelings but not be true feelings. For example, feeling "abandoned" and feeling "rejected" are not true feelings. These words seem to imply a feeling, but the statements are more like thoughts about another's behavior. In these kinds of statements, there is probably a genuine feeling of sadness or anger.

Nonviolent Communication (*NVC*) maintains that feelings are caused by our needs and by our thoughts, not by other people. This is not to say that what other people do to us is insignificant. According to *NVC*, other people may stimulate or trigger feelings in us through their actions. This is different than saying that they cause our feelings. When people act in a certain way, we create stories or have thoughts about those actions. The stories or thoughts that we create can lead to feelings. Just as others are not responsible for our feelings, we cannot hold ourselves responsible for the feelings of others. Although few of us can control our feelings as well as we want, the feelings are still manufactured within ourselves.

Using *NVC* language, we can avoid blaming others for our feelings. We can use the words, "I feel (name a feeling) because I need (name a need)." For example, "I feel sad because I need respect." Such a statement makes it clear that the feeling is due to our need, not to the actions of the other person. We want to avoid saying that "I feel (name a feeling) because you...." This type of statement can easily lead to defensiveness. If we speak using *NVC* language, others can listen to us with less defensiveness.

When we are feeling particularly anxious or upset, it is difficult to be attentive to others and to support them. Consequently, paying attention to our feelings is valuable. Noticing our feelings is not always easy and may take considerable practice to do consistently. When we are in the midst of a difficult interaction with another person, we can stop and ask ourselves how we are feeling.

Now is a good time to check in with your own feelings. So take a moment to stop and ask yourself how you are feeling. Maybe you are frustrated? Or are you afraid? Annoyed? Relaxed? Angry? And how did you feel during a recent interaction with your child who was demonstrating anger? Are you willing to begin a regular practice of noticing and naming your feelings when you are under stress? Are you willing to take responsibility for your feelings, rather than blaming another person?

5.

Notice Your Needs

Now that we have noticed our feelings (one component of self-empathy), we will turn our attention to the other component of self-empathy: the needs that contribute to our feelings. Needs are the longings that all people seek to fulfill. At one time or another, we all long for rest, a sense of belonging, a desire to contribute, freedom, autonomy, and so many other things. A way to tell if something we desire is a true need is to ask ourselves if every person would long for that at one time or another. Rest, food, and movement are examples of physical needs. Psychological needs include (among others) autonomy, freedom, community, and belonging. Rosenberg (2003) provided a more comprehensive list of common needs. But no list is complete; there are always additional words that can be added to a list.

It is common to confuse needs with strategies. There are many ways to meet our needs. Strategies are the ways that we can fulfill a need. But while we all have the same needs, we use different strategies for meeting these needs. For example, we can meet a need for belonging by strategies such as joining a team, signing up for a club, volunteering for a cause, or attending religious services. When one strategy does not work for us, we can always move on to another strategy. We are never dependent on a single strategy to meet our needs. It is very easy to confuse needs with strategies. In spoken or written language, we say things such as, "I really need a job." Although a job may be highly desirable, a job is not found on a list of needs. After all, a job is a way of acquiring money to be used for purchasing things like food, shelter, and recreation. A job is really a strategy, because there are other ways to get those needs for food, shelter, and recreation met.

Because there are many ways that we can meet a given need, we can get our needs met even if a particular person does not help us. And if we expect a particular person to fulfill our need, then we are making a demand of that person; demanding is not conducive to cooperative interactions.

We will also want to meet our needs through a variety of sources, rather than expecting the children before us to meet those needs. If we find that our need for respect is frequently unsatisfied, then we can identify other ways to experience respect. Our interactions with children are only one way to meet that need. There are so many other ways, and we will want to consider those ways if we are not getting the need met by our interactions with children. To be less affected by children's behavior, we have to know there are many strategies to meet our own needs.

We can note how well our needs are met. If our needs are satisfied, then we are likely to experience pleasant feelings. We are then in a position to be present for others. If our needs are not satisfied, then we are likely to experience unpleasant feelings that make it a challenge to be present for others. When we feel anxious or overwhelmed, for example, it can be very difficult to be emotionally available for others.

What needs of yours are pressing for your attention right now? Stop and reflect before continuing.

If you could use assistance in gaining this insight, you can ask yourself how satisfied you are with various common needs. For example, consider how satisfied your needs are for each of the following: rest, physical well-being, physical comfort, health, belonging, acceptance, community, self-expression, personal growth, and fun.

Sometimes we can use extra help in getting empathy (i.e., identifying our feelings and needs). We may not always be able to do this by ourselves. At such times, it can be very helpful to talk over our feelings with another person who can listen and help us to clarify our feelings and needs.

In sum, our feelings are tools to help us identify our needs. Children who are acting out their anger often trigger our own needs for respect, dignity, consideration, safety, and effectiveness. By getting in touch with our needs, we can say to ourselves, "I am really sad that this child called another child stupid. I really value respect. How else can I satisfy my need for respect?" It is okay to say, "I really want to do my job well. And I am so frustrated that this child is making that difficult by frequently calling out in class. How else can I experience effectiveness?" We can say to ourselves, "I really want to keep my children safe. And I am so scared that my child is punching the wall. How can I maintain safety?" In these statements, can you see the need as well as the feeling being expressed? It is not that we have to say these statements aloud. It is enough to say them to ourselves to get in touch with our feelings and needs.

As you recall an incident when your child lost his or her temper or expressed anger in a way that you did not like, what needs of yours do you notice? Are you willing to take time on a regular basis to notice your needs, especially during a challenging interaction with another person? Are you willing to take responsibility for satisfying those needs? What are some needs that are a challenge for you to satisfy?

6.

Notice Your Judgments

We have now discussed feelings as well as needs. An interesting thing can happen when we are not aware of our needs and feelings. That is, we can make judgments. And when we make judgments about others *being bad* or *doing something bad*, we tend to get angry. When we make judgments about ourselves, that anger directed inward generally becomes guilt or shame. When we experience anger, guilt, or shame, we can infer that we have made a judgment.

As a result of guilt or shame, we believe that the way to keep from doing something "wrong" again is to punish ourselves. Similarly, as a result of anger toward others, we believe that the way to stop others is to punish them.

Rosenberg (2003) pointed out the importance of the reasons for our behavior. Ideally, we want the reasons for our behavior to be as follows: to meet our needs and to contribute to meeting the needs of others. Such contributions to others' needs satisfy an important need of ours. If our strategy missed the mark, by connecting with our feelings and needs, we are in a position to choose a new strategy without relying on guilt and shame tactics. Whatever it was that we did, we were trying to meet a need. We are always doing our best (with the information that we have) to meet our needs. If we met one need but not another, then we can feel sad about our chosen strategy. We can then choose a new strategy for the future. Breaking the cycle of self-punishment is important for our well-being, and it will help us to have compassion for children with strong emotions.

By being aware of the needs that were left unfulfilled by our actions as well as the needs that were satisfied by our actions, we can experience true mourning or sadness for those actions. Furthermore, when we are in touch with those needs, we will be less likely to use guilt or shame to punish ourselves. We will be able to take effective action.

For example, we may notice judging ourselves because of how we handled a situation with a child. Maybe we spoke more loudly than we would have liked and threatened a consequence when our child was hanging upside down on the playground equipment. We yelled for the child to "get down before we go straight home and lose playground time for a month." Suppose that we think that we acted harshly. And maybe we are experiencing critical thoughts of ourselves for our actions. When we become aware of this judgment, we can seek to identify the needs we were trying to meet by our actions. Maybe we were trying to protect the child from injury. Maybe we were seeking safety. All needs are life-enhancing, so we can appreciate the value of the need for safety. It can help to experience the positive feelings that come from this intention. With these positive feelings, we are now more able to consider the needs that were not satisfied by our actions. We were scared, and our first instinct was to yell. By our actions, the child became scared and started to cry from a fear of the consequences and of us. Upon reflection, we realize our need for connection was not met. We can reflect on our desire for connection and allow ourselves to feel the sadness. The end result of focusing on both our needs for safety and connection awakens us to our humanness. This type of focusing can transform guilt to ordinary sadness that can dissolve and ultimately motivate us to consider new ways of acting in future situations.

In sum, we can notice our judgments about our actions. Then we can identify the needs that fuel the judgment, as well as the needs that are satisfied by the behavior we demonstrated. We can then briefly pause to reflect on all of those needs.

We tend to be very tough on ourselves. We make self-judgments by telling ourselves that we are selfish, impatient, and so many other negative words. We also tell ourselves that we *should* do certain things to be acceptable people. These statements set us up to experience guilt and shame. And once guilt comes, we believe that we deserve to be punished. When we tell ourselves that we have to do something, or we *should* do something out of a moralistic obligation, then we are undermining our own self-acceptance.

Developing a strong acceptance of oneself is powerful protection against the feelings that may be triggered by children who say and do things that we do not like. A belief that we are unconditionally worthy of acceptance, rather than bad or flawed, helps to buffer against the child's attempts to tell us otherwise.

Sometimes others judge us first, which triggers our own self-judgment. When that happens, it is very challenging to hear the other person's anger. We will be seeing how beneficial it is to be able to hear that anger. But if we start to judge ourselves in the process, and we become defensive due to our self-judgment, then communication breaks down. At such times, it helps to notice and be with our own feelings and needs.

Coping with judgments is a skill that we will be using on ourselves and with children. We can even model this important skill for children by vocalizing aloud our processes. This demonstration of empathy toward ourselves is effective in teaching children to be compassionate with themselves.

So far, we have been focused on judgments toward oneself. Let's take an example of a judgment we might make toward another person. When Jade teases a classmate for his clothing, the teacher finds herself getting angry. The anger lets her know she has made a judgment. She asks herself what that judgment is. She realizes that she views the child as *mean*. Remember, a judgment means that there is an unsatisfied need. So what is the need? As she reflects, the teacher realizes that her needs are for compassion and cooperation. She then pauses to experience the positive value of these needs. By doing so, she remembers that she wants to act in accordance with those needs instead of against them. We can also try to figure out what needs of Jade's are being met by her behavior. Once we understand these needs and see that the behavior is just a misguided attempt to meet the needs, we are in a more compassionate state of mind.

Sometimes when we are interacting with another person, our feelings are so intense that we need to stop ourselves from taking action that is likely to add fuel to the fire. In other words, we strive not to act out of anger. We can pause and reconnect with an intention to create an environment of collaboration with others. We can also use a self-calming practice to help us return to inner peace. We can take a few deep breaths and connect to what we are feeling and needing. Using this process that was described by Rosenberg (2003) supports the calming needed to continue relating positively to the other person.

Interacting with an angry child who is exhibiting challenging behavior can trigger our judgments. Owning our feelings and needs in such moments helps to keep us from engaging in hostile actions toward children. And once again, it is worthwhile to learn these valuable skills before we are faced with a child who is angry.

Are you willing to notice your judgments and to recognize your own unsatisfied needs that are behind these judgments? Can you recall a time when you acted toward your upset child in a way that you regret? What needs of yours were met and not met by your action? Without rushing, try to experience the power of those needs, the ones met as well as the ones not met. If this is too difficult to do by yourself, do you have someone who can help you with this?

7.

Model Respect

An effective way to teach people a life skill is to model the skill. We are much more influential when we use our actions to show what we believe in than when we use our words in the form of lecturing or advice-giving. Respectful behavior is a life skill that is worth modeling for young people.

Respect is an important need of ours, and we can easily get angry if respect is not given to us. Respect is something we are told is to be given to elders, to our parents, and to people of status. Does giving respect to a child even make sense? Does it make even less sense to give respect to a child who has triggered our anger?

We can easily understand the anger that adults may feel when they experience a lack of respect from children. If children are triggering this anger, then it can be especially challenging to act with the best of intentions toward them. Our anger can trigger urges to punish. We may have the thought that such children who show inadequate respect to us do not deserve our consideration. However, it is partially because children are not adequately experiencing self-respect that it is so difficult for them to give respect to others.

Respect is so critical to the other strategies described in this guide that a brief discussion of it is in order. Children's "disrespectful" behavior is often an attempt, sometimes a desperate one, to experience respect. When children's emotions are not acknowledged and they are treated with hostility for their attempts to seek respect, the self-perpetuating cycle is triggered.

As pointed out by Hart and Kindle Hodson (2006), treating children with a lack of respect can lead to their lacking a sense of emotional safety. Reducing emotional safety is especially problematic for children with pre-existing trauma. When children experience threats to emotional safety, they must find ways of coping. In contrast, when children feel safe, they are eager to explore, learn, and take risks. We can connect much better with children if we speak with respect toward them.

To thrive, children need to be accepted despite their actions. Although few of us are likely to get such unconditional acceptance, those who learn that they are essentially bad are more prone to difficulties. Certain words suggest a lack of acceptance. When children are told that they "must" or "better" do something in order not to face punishment, their anxiety is usually stimulated. Many children can tolerate this anxiety. With some children, however, the result can be shutting down or outbursts.

The challenging behavior that we see in many children is a reflection of their sense of powerlessness. They have turned this powerlessness from a passive form into an active form, and they now express it as a behavioral habit in their interpersonal interactions. Children need to learn that they will not be met with disregard. We need to show basic respect even to children who show little respect to us.

Conventional thinking is that children who "disrespect" others must be punished and shamed. This strategy tends to backfire, as the anger that builds up within these children will lead to even greater disrespect in the future. Showing respect to a child who has triggered frustration or anger can be a sign that the adult has a strong self-concept and is able to effectively withstand the child's anger.

It is common to treat children without the same respect that we give adults. And then we are surprised when children do not seem to respect us. Sometimes adults are so frustrated with a child that the child is literally dragged or pulled. Years ago, it was common for children to be pulled by their ears as an expression of the adult's anger. In such interactions, children learn that they lack status. The anger that may develop in these children is likely to come out in some form at a later moment, even if the punishing adult does not witness it.

When children witness respectful interactions, including respect given to them, they have the opportunity to reconsider their own power-driven interactions. When the respectful interactions that these children witness end in satisfactory outcomes, namely both parties meeting their needs, the chances are still greater that the children will transform their own patterns of behavior. A person who shows respect helps the receiver of that respect to remain calm and ultimately respectful in turn. This is a powerful strategy in interactions with children prone to intense or frequent anger.

Things we can do that are not consistent with respecting children include yelling at them to scare them, making excessive demands of them, punishing them harshly, and criticizing them. This does not mean that adults cannot express themselves when children's actions are upsetting to them. In addition, it does not mean that we cannot set limits on behavior. There are effective ways of doing that with respect, and we will address those in a later chapter.

8.

Make Requests Rather Than Demands

Adults often think it is the job of children to comply or follow directions. When children do not do as directed, they are often labeled as noncompliant. There is a great deal of professional literature on teaching compliance to children. Stickers, stars, or tokens are often a part of this goal. Furthermore, these external reinforcers may even interfere with the child's natural desire to do what is being asked. But is there any alternative to compliance, when it comes to children's behavior?

Conventional advice is for adults to make clear commands to children. However, such commands can sometimes contribute to a child's defiance. In addition, when adults make commands, it tends to lead to similar power displays in children's behavior. Commanding is very similar to demanding, and we usually want children to give up their own demandingness. Yet conventional advice preaches that we tell children to do what we say, rather than what we do.

We often command children to do things that are in their best interests, instead of helping them see the value behind the request. In contrast, we can work with the child to put both the adult's needs and the child's needs on the table. This helps children learn that everyone's needs matter equally. Consequently, they receive a valuable model of cooperation.

When an adult tells a child to do something, without being open to the child's reaction, the child is likely to experience some resistance. For some children, this resistance may be demonstrated in a variety of behavior issues. Children want to participate in making the decisions that affect them. Instead of compliance, a more useful goal may be cooperation.

We can often make use of children's natural tendency to cooperate by asking them (rather than demanding) for something that we would like. Some children may cooperate simply due to an inherent desire to connect with others. If the child sees the value behind the request, the likelihood of cooperation increases further.

We can make requests using the same respectful approach an adult would use when asking a respected person for something. There is a prevalent notion that it is children's responsibility to comply with adults. However, there is value in choice, and we ultimately want children to act based on the inherent value of their actions.

From the perspective of *NVC*, a request has several elements. First of all, we ask the person to do something rather than NOT to do something. Framing the request in this way also makes it easier for children to know what is being asked of them. Second, requests involve asking for something that the child is able to do. If the request is beyond the child's cognitive or physical capacity, then we are likely to be met with a negative response. A third element of a request is to ask for concrete actions that the child can do in the moment. Putting together just the first three elements, we would ask Jill to take her sibling to a movie, rather than asking her to stop bothering the sibling. A fourth element of a request is that we are willing to hear "no" as an answer. If we get angry when the request is not met with a "yes," we have really made a demand. When an adult makes a true request, the child has the option of saying "no" without getting into trouble.

Adults making requests are well-served to get into a frame of mind in which they are unattached to the result and can tolerate hearing "no" from the child. The goal is for the child to respond with a "yes" only if the child wants to say "yes." If the child wants to say "no," we would not want the child to say "yes" just to avoid punishment.

If the child says "no," we can gently seek further understanding of the child's needs related to the request. If we show an empathic understanding of what prevents the child from doing as we asked, then we can promote the likelihood of eventual cooperation. We can eventually seek an agreement that meets everyone's needs.

To further promote cooperation, it can be beneficial for children to participate in the creation of rules and agreements. Their participation helps to prevent resistance to abiding by these agreements.

One request that we can make to children with anger issues is to verbally express their frustration to us before taking matters into their hands (by striking someone, using profanity, or using any behavioral expression that leads to further difficulties). We can ask children (who are prone to anger problems) to tell us the feelings they are experiencing at such moments. In the classroom, the teacher can establish a nonverbal signal for the child to communicate the need for a moment with the teacher. This technique can allow for some privacy in the dialogue. Although this approach may be inconvenient to the teacher, the alternative is a child who loses self-control and has an outburst that is more disruptive than the verbalization of feelings. In this light, the inconvenience of the brief verbal exchange seems more satisfactory.

In some situations, especially in a classroom setting with many children, adults may find requests to be rather inefficient and inconvenient. We are better off deciding in advance whether we require immediate compliance or if we would merely appreciate the child's cooperation. When we are not in conflict with children and we have built rapport with them, commands or clear instructions may be appropriate in order to direct children to begin and end activities. We may also choose to give instructions if it is very important to the adult that the child immediately do something or if the child is engaged in a behavior that could cause harm to people or property. At such times, we can minimize the negative impact of commands by following a few guidelines: issuing the commands in a neutral or polite manner (even using the word *please*); making commands brief and uncomplicated; avoiding unnecessary verbalization after the command; and giving children at least five seconds to comply before we assume they are not complying.

In matters of physical protection, we must also sometimes make demands of children by setting limits on them. There may be some occasions when adults need to make decisions on behalf of the child. When children are using physical aggression, for example, we may need to use force to protect others. In other situations, as well, there may be times when we want to set limits to protect the rights and needs of others. In addition, we may sometimes need to protect children from themselves by setting limits on them. However, we can usually attempt to gain their cooperation well before the situation has reached this point.

Although it would be far better to limit the amount of control we exert over children, adults sometimes do not have the luxury of seeking cooperation. When control is necessary, we can minimize the negative impact on children by empathizing with their feelings related to our demand. This topic will be addressed further in the discussion of empathy in a later chapter.

9.

Have Fun Together

By engaging in pleasurable activities and having fun with our children, we can further our rapport with them, provide stress relief, and remind them that we value their need for fun. By accomplishing these things, we can help to keep their emotions on the more positive side. Furthermore, we can make it less likely that they will have anger reactions.

One valuable strategy to create fun, pleasurable experiences is through playful interactions with children. Toward that end, games and play can be used to create fun opportunities. When an adult and a child play games of the child's choice, the child usually enjoys the feeling that comes from choice. This is a simple way to balance the loss of power that children often feel in those instances in which adults must use their power over children.

During play, children can ideally choose from a variety of fun activities that are acceptable to the adult. The adult can enjoy the game as well. And the play allows the opportunity for the adult to model respectful behavior for the child.

In addition to play, we can provide other pleasurable experiences for children. Such experiences, of course, vary by age but can include going to the park, riding bicycles together, working on a puzzle together, going out for a meal or snack, going on a trip to the zoo or an amusement park, watching a movie or television show together, reading a story together, going to a sporting event together, or going boating or fishing.

In the school setting, pleasurable experiences can be created through playing classroom games. There are many books available on such classroom games. One example is *Great Group Games* by Ragsdale and Saylor (2007). Classroom games can add student involvement to potentially tedious tasks like memorizing facts. Games also help people get comfortable with each other, create opportunities for learning, and allow children to practice social skills.

10.

Encourage Contribution

Contribution is a basic need of humans. A rewarding experience, contribution comes naturally to us. It can be easier to see this if you think of how you feel when you do something for another person. The joy of contribution can also be taken away if it is forced upon us, and we are doing something out of a sense of obligation.

Children's contributions are sometimes taken for granted. And they are often pressured into doing things that they do not want to do. We can turn this around by helping children to experience their contributions as meaningful to us. We can do this by expressing our appreciation for their contributions. We can also begin to view the child's cooperative behavior as a form of contribution that we can appreciate and encourage.

Instead of simply thanking the child, we can report our feelings. We can also report the needs that are satisfied within us by the child's behavior. For example, "When I see that you cleaned your room, I am very relieved. Now I know you will be safe from tripping when you get out of bed in the middle of the night." Or, "I am thrilled by this gift from you, because I will have so much fun using it."

We can harness the power of the joy of contribution by letting our children know how much we appreciate it when they have peacefully expressed their frustration (i.e., without acting it out in ways that are problematic for us). To do this successfully, we must decide how we wish children to express their anger. Once we are clear on what types of statements and actions we prefer from children, we can then begin to encourage such behavior.

A good place to begin is to encourage children to verbalize upsetting feelings to us. When we notice the child has verbalized such feelings, we can express our appreciation for the child's contribution to the peacefulness of the environment. We speak to children about what we value in terms of their completed actions, rather than what we wish they would do. In other words, instead of focusing on negative behaviors, we notice as soon as they have expressed feelings. We then say that we are pleased with their self-expression. Although this process takes a little time and effort, I believe it is preferable to an anger outburst.

Each of three elements is important in using this process to effectively contribute to behavior change. We need to encourage immediately, repeatedly, and consistently. By doing so, we can provide (what behaviorists view as) positive reinforcement. To be more specific, we can best encourage children by letting them know their contributions as soon as possible after their actions. In addition, we can best encourage children by letting them know over and over again each time they contribute. Use of a nonverbal signal to accent the appreciation adds to the effectiveness of this process. Depending on the setting and the relationship, a handshake, high five, or thumbs up may be appropriate. We would show some enthusiasm even with older children as we encourage them. With younger children, it helps to add extra enthusiasm in our voices as we demonstrate our appreciation.

When children have well-established patterns of adaptive expression of their anger, we can begin to express our encouragement less consistently. However, we need to be consistent as we are helping them to develop new habits.

In contrast to our verbally appreciating the child's contribution (through our expression of our feelings and our satisfied needs), other statements may not have the same positive impact. Consider comments such as "Good job" or "You're fantastic." Even though these comments are positive, they do not inform children of the adult needs that were satisfied by the behavior. As a result, children may not know the important contributions that they have made.

When a child does not have the skills to perform the behavior of calmly expressing his or her feelings, we need to break this difficult task into smaller steps. By our expressing our appreciation of these smaller steps, the child will eventually perform the larger behavior. There are several ways to accomplish this task.

We can step in before the outburst has occurred and express appreciation for the child's self-restraint (even if the child would likely have lost his temper, seconds later). We can encourage the child by saying something like, "I am so pleased that you hesitated for a few seconds when you were angry. I know that one day you will even be able to calmly talk about your feelings of frustration and anger. I really value the peacefulness that you are working toward." We could also prompt children to report their feelings during moments of frustration, rather than waiting for them to report feelings on their own. Finally, we could encourage children when they remember to use their self-calming practices.

We can vary the way we express our encouragement of a child's contribution. We would not want the child to hear the same words over and over. We would like the child to hear the genuineness of our gratitude. For practical purposes, we may sometimes decide to shorten our verbal expressions of appreciation. We can still accomplish the objective by the following statement: "I am glad you used your calming breaths. Thanks for keeping the peace." In the example, notice the feeling of gladness and the need of peace.

What other behaviors could your children use as substitutes for the challenging behaviors they already tend to use? Taking each replacement behavior into consideration, can you identify any smaller steps that the child could perform to pave the way for this replacement behavior?

We want to give children much practice at performing these positive replacement behaviors and the smaller steps along the way to the full replacement behaviors. More practice means more opportunities for us to provide encouragement. Therefore, we have to allow children many situations in which they can show us what they are learning to do.

Contributions include more than just replacement behaviors for challenging behaviors. Contributions can include acts of service. Contributions can also include talents and interests that are used to add joy to the lives of others. Children's interests can be encouraged and nurtured, so that they see their potential gifts. If they enjoy art and it is encouraged and appreciated, children will come to use their art to contribute to others.

It can be beneficial to help children to develop a positive vision of the future. This vision provides hope and prevents despair, and it can be encouraged by adults who show enthusiasm for children's interests and strengths. Talking with children about their interests validates them and establishes rapport. Asking them what they want to be when grown up, or what their goals are, can stimulate a discussion of the ways they can contribute through their actions.

11.

Lower Stress or Prepare for It

By keeping children from being overwhelmed with excessive stress, we make it less likely that they will experience anger. Although some stress is unavoidable and probably adaptive, it is important to realize when stress is becoming too great for children. Sometimes it is difficult to know where to draw the line. In the case of children who are prone to frequent displays of anger, it is especially important to be attentive to their stress levels.

As a simple example, we would not want to put pressure on these children to achieve straight A's in school. The stress could be too much, and the likelihood of an outburst would be increased. Of course, we can encourage effort and provide support to help the child achieve to his or her potential.

Another example is refraining from overscheduling children with anger issues. On top of school, homework, and organized recreational activities, children need time for free play. Overscheduling them puts excessive stress on them.

Lowering demands to realistic levels is not the same as setting the bar low for the child. We can expect children to put forth effort, but we cannot expect everyone to excel in everything.

Can you think of any examples of excessive pressure on a child having anger issues? How can you help to lower the demands on the child?

We can prevent some stressful situations that are likely to overwhelm children. However, other stressful situations may be important for children to face. After all, if we avoid all stressful situations, we will miss out on many life opportunities. When we do not want children to miss out on important opportunities that may be stressful, we can help greatly by preparing children for the upcoming situation. In doing so, we can describe what is likely to happen, express our confidence in their abilities to meet the stress, practice the calming response that we have taught them, and discuss their concerns.

What stressful situations does your child need to face, without your lowering the demands? What can you say to the child to help prepare him or her?

12.

Be a Problem-Solving Partner

Another preventive tool that we can provide to children is guidance in how to think through social problems. In her book on Interpersonal Cognitive Problem-Solving (ICPS, for short), Myrna Shure (1992) described the use of a process for teaching children to evaluate their own solutions to interpersonal problems. The process encourages children to come up with many possible ways that they could respond to problems that they are having with others. This brainstorming step allows children to consider all options that enter their minds.

For example, William can be helped to identify all the actions he could take if a peer were challenging him to a fight. In doing so, he should be encouraged to come up with as many options as he can. He identifies responses such as accepting the fight, trying to befriend the child, and telling a teacher at school.

Can your child identify a problem about which to brainstorm a variety of solutions? How many solutions can the child identify?

After these multiple options have been listed, we can teach children to consider each option one by one, including the consequences that are likely to go with each option. The child may come up with several possible responses, some better and some worse. For example, William may decide that the consequences of accepting the challenge to a fight could result in getting suspended from school, not to mention getting hurt.

The consequences of telling a teacher at school could result in the children making peace or the other child getting angrier. On the other hand, the consequences of trying to befriend the other child, by calmly listening to the other child's issues, could result in peace between them.

After considering the possible consequences of the various potential solutions, the child can be helped to decide on a behavioral option. In our example, William may decide to try to befriend this other child.

If there was a recent behavioral episode, it can be useful to review the incident from a problem-solving perspective. This process involves reviewing the events that occurred before the child's behavior, the child's actual behavior that occurred, the consequences of the child's behavior, and other behavioral options that were available to the child (along with possible consequences of such options). Sometimes children also anticipate a difficult, upcoming interpersonal situation. At such times, they often need help in considering how to handle the situation.

This problem-solving process encourages a partnership between adults and children in discovering possible solutions, considering potential consequences, and deciding on future courses of action.

The ICPS curriculum would ideally be standard for children with chronic behavioral problems from anger, but other children could benefit from this curriculum as well. It is important to note that children are taught during times of peace, rather than during behavioral episodes. At times of peace, we are more able to consider alternatives.

Greene (2014) described, and illustrated in detail, a three-part problem-solving process that adults can use with children to address adult concerns about a child's behavior.

An initial step is for the adult to report his or her observations of the child's behavior. The adult also seeks an understanding of the child's perspective on the situation. The adult maintains a patient and curious attitude to encourage a full expression by the child.

After the child expresses his or her perspective, the adult expresses his or her own concerns related to the child's behavior. Finally, the adult encourages the child to work together to find a mutually satisfying solution to the problem.

To use a simplified example, let's suppose a child is having difficulty completing her homework. After the father reports his observations, the child's perspective is sought. The girl reveals that the homework is boring and that she would rather avoid it.

In this example, the father expresses a concern that the child will have difficulties on the test if she does not complete homework. Possibly the child's grade will be reduced as well for not doing the homework.

As the father invites the child to find a mutually satisfying solution, the girl identifies a solution to work for short periods of time with frequent breaks so that she can maintain enthusiasm. (The reader can consult Greene's book for additional examples and aspects of this process.)

Using concepts from *NVC*, we can also highlight the needs of the girl as part of the problem-solving process. The girl has an apparent need for mental stimulation (which is not satisfied by the homework). The father also helps the girl to identify her own needs for learning, growth, and challenge. Because her behavior involves avoiding the homework, her behavior is not satisfying the latter set of needs. By helping the girl to notice her unsatisfied needs, her father can help to motivate her to engage in a problem-solving process.

Along the way, we can use the ICPS steps of generating multiple solutions, evaluating possible consequences, and picking a solution.

By resolving these conflicts together, the child learns that the adult is a valuable resource and need not be viewed as a threat. This process contributes to the cooperation and mutual respect that minimize the likelihood of childhood anger outbursts.

Does your child demonstrate behaviors that you would like to bring to his or her attention? What words can you use to elicit the child's perspective on his or her behavior? After the child's perspective is expressed, how can you express your concerns to the child? Finally, how can you invite the child to engage in a process of working together to solve the problem?

Part III

After Anger,
Before Behavioral Escalation

For children who often display physical aggression, defiance, or other behavioral expressions of anger, it is worthwhile to prevent unnecessary instances of anger. Despite all efforts to prevent a child from experiencing this emotion, anger sometimes happens. Before behavior deteriorates, there are steps that can be taken to de-escalate emotions and to prevent acting-out behaviors.

13.

Empathize First, Problem-Solve Second

Empathy with children who are upset involves taking the time to help them to identify their feelings and the underlying needs behind those feelings. It will involve listening deeply to hear the child's innermost intent. By using empathic listening, we can help create an atmosphere of caring and positive problem-solving. Empathy is a key component of *Nonviolent Communication*.

When properly used, empathy conveys the listener's acceptance of the speaker's inner state. Getting the child's point of view out in the open is critical to a problem-solving process that will occur at a later time.

In order to clarify what empathy is, we need to know what empathy is not. These non-empathic responses are common ways that people respond to emotional messages. The intention behind these non-empathic responses may be good, and these types of responses can be very tempting alternatives for us to use. These alternative responses may even be very helpful under some circumstances. But these alternatives have an entirely different effect than empathy does. And empathy is a very effective way of helping the child who has begun to experience anger, before behavioral escalation has occurred. Here are examples of what empathy is not.

Empathy is not advice-giving.

Empathy is not reassuring the child, even if there is intention of comforting him or her.

Empathy is not minimizing the child's feelings by telling him or her that the situation is "not that big a deal."

Empathy is not sympathy or statements such as "You poor baby!"

Empathy is not about distracting children from their concerns.

Empathy is not about analyzing or diagnosing the child's issues.

Empathy is not about telling stories of what we lived through.

And it certainly is not about judging children for their feelings or actions.

It is challenging to change our established communication habits. Furthermore, it may not seem natural to give empathy, especially when we are used to other methods of communication. But new habits can be formed, and empathy can eventually become a preferred style of communicating with an angry child.

We will likely be unable to effectively give empathy if we are very upset. In such instances, we will probably find it difficult to give the emotional space needed by the child. At such times, we can take time apart from the child, literally or figuratively, to regroup and provide comfort to ourselves.

Now that we understand what empathy is not, let's further clarify what empathy is.

Empathy is about attending to feelings and the underlying needs that contribute to those feelings.

Empathy involves an understanding that we all have feelings and that no feeling is wrong.

Empathy involves giving space to the child so that he or she can experience the feeling without rushing through it.

Having already provided self-comforting, we are now ready to listen and assist the child before us. Using the process of empathy, we will help the child to notice any feelings (and the needs that contribute to those feelings). If the child has already begun self-expression, or if we have a clue as to the answer, we can seek to elicit feelings from the child by asking,

"Are you (name a feeling)?" We can safely ask most children if they are upset. This is a useful word, because it is vague enough to elicit a "yes" response most of the time. With a positive response to this question, we have been primed for a more specific feeling guess. We can then guess a more targeted feeling, such as *angry* or *sad*. We typically pose the phrase as a guess, so that the child can respond "yes" or "no."

When we see a snarled expression on the child's face, we may ask, "Are you angry?" Our strategy is to make all feelings acceptable. By asking if the child is feeling angry, we seek to convey that even anger is acceptable.

If the child goes into the story of what happened, or what another person did to him or her, we can try to paraphrase or summarize what we hear the child saying. This summarizing process is sometimes referred to as a reflection of the child's words. The child may also give us his or her opinions and judgments of others. Summarizing these opinions and judgments can show the child that we are listening with concern. However, we do not want to agree with these judgments. By showing the child that we truly want to listen, the child may be more willing to reveal personal feelings. After reflecting, we can then guess the child's feeling. Again, we generally ask, rather than tell children, how they are feeling. It is helpful to have this one-to-one dialogue with the child away from noise and distractions.

We may also notice an observable behavior of a child (such as balling up a fist or slamming down an object) and point it out to the child without judgment or anger in our voices. We can say, "When you (state the child's observable behavior), I wonder if you are angry....Are you?" (This statement is best used before there has been a dramatic escalation of behavior.) We can continue with, "Would you be willing to talk with me about your anger?" If escalation to destructiveness has begun, we will need to skip this step for the moment. (This scenario will be covered later.)

To accomplish the task of helping children to identify their feelings, it will be useful to teach them feeling words. We won't get far in our conversations with children until they have a basic vocabulary of feelings. Child therapists and school counselors often have posters of children making various facial expressions to teach children how to identify their feelings.

Having helped to identify their feelings, we also want to help children identify the psychological needs underneath. We discussed needs in an earlier chapter, and you may recall that all people have needs. Just as we accepted their feelings, we want to accept their needs (for example, respect, choice, freedom, and acceptance). We may ask, "Do you want (name the specific need)?"

As we learn to identify our own feelings and needs, it becomes easier to notice and accept the feelings and needs of children. When we become especially skilled, which can take a good amount of practice, we may reach a point at which we often "see through" the behavior of children to their feelings and needs.

Children's actions, as frustrating as they may be to the adults who care for these children, can all be seen as attempts to meet needs. Given the strategies that are at their disposal, children's actions reflect what they believe will best meet their needs. Sometimes the strategies that children (and adults) use are in conflict with our wishes. So naturally it makes sense for us to experience frustration. It also makes sense that we may experience sadness when children's actions are in conflict with what we wish. We would be wise not to express overt hostility if children do not oblige us, and we can seek to guide their actions without our showing hostility.

Just as the child needs to learn to name feelings, it is important to develop a vocabulary of needs. Rosenberg (2003) listed a variety of needs. Although the names of some needs on the list can be very abstract and difficult, it is okay to change the words to make them more child-friendly. For children who experience strong anger, needs like respect, choice, and freedom are big ones. Other important needs may include autonomy, belonging, play, acceptance, physical well-being, and peace. Many people find it helpful to have a copy of a needs list available to pick the appropriate need, when trying to connect emotionally with others and with oneself.

When a child is experiencing a surge of strong emotions, the left side of the brain (the verbal side) may be unable to be engaged at the moment. Connecting with the right side of the brain, by using body language that conveys calmness and acceptance, is as important as the words that we use.

When children do not do what we ask them to do, it is helpful to find out what they are alternatively seeking. In *Nonviolent Communication*, the expression commonly used is to hear the "yes" behind the "no." By being attuned to what children are seeking, we can learn what underlying needs they are attempting to meet. So when a child does not want to do what we are asking, we can ask questions to find out what the child needs. For example, suppose we ask David to clean his room. When he does not oblige us, we can guess, "Do you need to relax a little?" Another option we have is to express our own feelings and needs. (How to express ourselves will be discussed in an upcoming chapter.) Expressing ourselves is usually less effective when a child is experiencing strong emotion.

A commonly used approach to the "no" given by children is to impose a consequence of some kind in order to cause the child pain, suffering, or sadness. Such consequences can include yelling at a child, threatening the child, or spanking the child. These tactics are not consistent with the approach I am suggesting. We would not want to issue consequences in order to cause pain. And an over-reliance on punishing consequences is not conducive to harmonious interactions, especially with children who are prone to anger outbursts.

When we rely heavily on these strategies, we can expect children to lie in order to avoid getting into trouble with the adult. We can also expect that the motivation of the child's behavior will be to avoid consequences, rather than to help meet the needs of others. We are well-served to use any limit-setting tactics with an attitude of compassion toward the child. We can express our reservations about the use of our tactics but proceed with the tactics using sensitivity to the child affected. More on setting limits will be discussed later.

When children tell us what they think of us, we want to be secure with who we are. By having this deep acceptance of ourselves, we will not be overly affected by their comments. For some of us, professional counseling may be needed to enhance our opinions of ourselves in order to achieve this goal. Instead of taking in the insulting words, we can listen for the feelings and needs behind the words. We can use the same empathic approach used when receiving the child's "no." We can ask, "Are you angry?" Then we can listen for the child's underlying psychological need.

Empathizing with others before educating them is a valuable concept. We want to resist lecturing children who are persistently triggering our emotions. These lectures fall on deaf ears, if the child is actively trying to meet a need that our strategy does not seem to meet. By the same token, we want to resist advising children without first asking if they are willing to listen.

Using empathy in response to a child's "no" (and in response to a child's comments that we do not like) is a major transition for most adults. It is easy to understand the frustration we might experience in giving up consequences, demands, and lectures. We may have received many cultural and family messages that such demands and lectures are proper techniques in raising children.

At times it is not necessary to speak aloud to children about their feelings and needs. Instead, we can silently show concern. While doing so, we can wonder about the child's feelings and needs.

It is valuable to establish a connection with each individual child. Individual meetings (one adult and one child) are helpful in doing so. It can be quite a challenge to apply this method to a large group of children who are all angry at the same time, such as in a classroom for children with behavioral challenges. Much preparation needs to be done through individual meetings with students and with their parents before the children can be taught as a group.

Let's demonstrate empathy for a child who is angry. David (D) was arguing with a classmate moments earlier. David's face reveals his emotion. His teacher (T) approaches David and pulls him aside after the teacher addresses the classmate.

T: David, I want to see how you are. Are you angry? (The teacher seeks to identify the student's feeling.)

D: Yeah, he doesn't want to be my friend anymore. I didn't even do anything.

T: Do you want to understand what happened between the two of you? (The teacher is attempting to help identify the student's need.)

D: He said he doesn't like it that I talk about him behind his back. I didn't even do it.

T: So you are mad that you are getting blamed for something you didn't even do. Maybe you want to be understood? (Being understood is a need that we all have. By bringing that need to the center of attention, there is the opportunity for a processing of emotions. The intensity of the anger can often be reduced.)

D: If he would just listen to me. (His anger is starting to change to sadness.)

T: I can see how important it is for you to be understood. Maybe the two of you can work this out.

As stated earlier, when we are triggered by children's behavior, we are not in a good place to provide empathy. At such times, we will usually find it helpful to give ourselves self-empathy. (Refer to the earlier chapters on this process.) This may require a temporary exit, either literal or figurative, after which we can return less triggered and more ready to empathize. In practice, we may need to move between self-empathy and empathy for the child, as well as expression of our own needs (to be discussed later) and problem-solving.

As an exercise, it is useful to reflect on several common scenarios in which a child is triggering some unpleasant feelings in us. For the exercise, we can ask ourselves what feelings and needs are going on within us. And then we can ask ourselves what feelings and needs may be going on within the child. A follow-up exercise is to consider how we may ask the child about his or her feelings and needs. Taking the time to do this exercise now and on a regular basis will help us to make these skills part of our new programming.

From personal experience, I know that it can be very challenging to speak in this language of empathy. It takes time and effort to learn. I have also found that a great deal of the benefit occurs from simply accepting the child's feelings and needs, even if we cannot accurately name them.

Having received empathy, the child who has been triggered by strong feelings is now calmer and more receptive to problem-solving. We can now use the same problem-solving skills discussed earlier. It is important not to jump to problem-solving before the child's feelings and needs have been validated.

Part IV

After Behavioral Escalation

When the child was calm and not in the midst of a triggered state, we modeled respect through our interactions with the child and with others. We emphasized cooperation over compliance. We helped the child to contribute, and we showed appreciation of the child's efforts by telling the child how he or she contributed to our needs. We made requests when possible, rather than overloading the child with demands. We had fun on a regular basis, playing games that the child got to choose.

We also considered whether the situation would exceed the child's capacity for coping. When we decided it probably would, we chose to protect the child from the situation until his or her coping capacity would be adequate to meet the situational demands.

We talked with the child about self-calming. We agreed to regularly practice so the child could use the calming strategies when upset. Such calming techniques may have included taking some deep breaths. The child was helped to imagine getting upset and then using the self-calming technique.

We also helped to prepare the child in advance for situations likely to be challenging. We helped the child to visualize the situation as it may unfold. We asked the child how he or she felt while visualizing the situation. We helped the child to practice the self-calming technique when feeling nervous during the visualization. Then we asked how the child might respond. We asked the child to consider many possible responses, and what the consequences may be for each of these responses.

However, not everything went according to plan. The child became angry when punched by a peer in the playground. Still, the child managed to make choices that met his or her needs for cooperation and safety. We gave the child empathy. Then we helped the child to decide on a course of action. In addition, the child went on to become friends with the child who punched him or her.

I have described an approach in which adults are listening actively, empathizing, modeling self-control, helping to problem-solve, and relying more on cooperation than control. By using this respectful approach, the likelihood of meltdowns will be significantly reduced.

However, meltdowns may still occur. Sometimes even our best efforts to prevent a situation from escalating are not successful. At this point, we have to mitigate the damages. The following steps are a guide for this process.

14.

Set Caring Limits

When children reach the point of getting so upset that they have outbursts or meltdowns, we can set limits while still showing sensitivity to their painful emotions. Children need us to be calm and caring when they have become this upset. They need to know that an adult is available even when they act out their anger. If they are open to it, we may even be able to guide them to use the self-calming techniques that we have previously taught them.

Let's take an example of a child who has knocked over a chair during a display of anger. A common reaction is to verbally scold the child and threaten with consequences. Instead, we can stay connected by saying, "I know you are angry now. I want to hear about that anger, but I would like you to take some deep breaths to help you calm down so we can talk. "

Some people may believe that giving attention of any form to children during anger outbursts reinforces the acting-out behaviors. However, children need the assurance that they are accepted and cared for, even when they are extremely upset and have lost self-control. Of course we do not want to let the meltdown force us to give in to the child's demands. However, by showing that we are present for the child and that we have not rejected him or her, we help to ensure that the child does not experience unnecessary shame.

With a young child, we may be able to interrupt the tantrum using simple distraction techniques. For a very young child, just showing a toy or turning on the television may stop the tantrum.

We certainly want to avoid escalating the tantrum by lecturing or punishing the child. We do no service to the child by yelling. Even discussion can be delayed until the tantrum is finished. It is wise to use the minimum control needed to protect people and property.

When children are extremely angry, they may sometimes lose self-control. In the midst of such outbursts, we may need to use physical force to protect the child from self-injury, to protect others, and to prevent destruction of property. When such force is used, it is for the purpose of protection rather than punishment.

If we are using force to protect the child, we may say to the child, "You're safe now. I want you to be safe." If we are using force to protect others, we may say, "We are all safe now. I want all of us to be safe." If we are using force to protect property from damage, we may say to the child, "You're safe here. And we have to respect people's property."

Sometimes it is necessary to help move the child to another location, if the location of the outburst interferes with other people's well-being. We want to show warmth and sensitivity in having to use such physical force. The interested reader can refer to other sources for learning how to physically restrain when necessary.

Later when the child is calmer, we can let the child know that we appreciate how he or she has calmed down.

15.

Attend to Your Own Feelings

Once a child's meltdown has begun, as well as when it is over, we want to be aware of our own feelings being stirred up within us. If we are in a public place, we may find it embarrassing. We may be upset or afraid. We may need to take a few deep breaths to calm ourselves.

After children have acted out, we may become angry as well. It is important to address our own anger. This involves simultaneously recognizing our anger, allowing it to exist without pushing it away, and refraining from losing self-control. A problem can occur if we act on our anger by losing our tempers or by trying to harm the people who triggered our anger. Consequently, it is beneficial to practice inhibiting our tendency to act at the moment we feel anger. This often involves taking a break from the situation so that we may calm ourselves.

Underneath anger is a more tender feeling, often sadness or fear. We can attempt to recognize these more tender feelings. By doing so, we can then experience a release of pain.

Our anger signals us that an important need of ours is not being met (Rosenberg, 2003). Instead of pushing away the anger, we can use the anger as a signal to help us identify that need of ours. If I find myself angry, I can take a few breaths, allowing myself to feel the anger. I can notice if there are any physical sensations within my body. I can wonder what need is unsatisfied, behind the anger. Maybe I notice an unsatisfied need for respect. Sometimes the anger may transform into other feelings.

Rather than acting out of our anger, we are best off acting out of our values. We can identify our values and then act in accordance with them, no matter how the child is behaving. Common values include acceptance, peace, love, respect, and compassion. Therefore, we may feel anger but act with love. For example, we may choose to address our anger by telling the child that we are very upset about the child's reaction and that we would like to figure out a way to learn from the experience, to keep it from happening again.

It is common for us adults to think that children have defeated us if they are not punished when they act out of anger. However, we will soon be seeing that we can respond more effectively if we do not act with the intention of causing them pain.

Take a moment to recall a time when a child you were caring for had a powerful anger outburst. How did you feel at that moment? Can you identify a need of yours that was unsatisfied at that moment?

16.

Refrain from Punishing

In the 1960s, Diana Baumrind, a research psychologist, found that parents who used an *authoritarian* approach to parenting experienced less satisfactory outcomes with their children than *authoritative* parents experienced with their children. The less-preferred authoritarian approach is characterized by high parental control with little room for discussion. These parents are strict disciplinarians. Often characterized as warm but firm, the more-preferred authoritative parenting style establishes high parental expectations for children but allows for discussion. These parents take the child's point of view into consideration. When children do not meet parental expectations, authoritative parents can be nurturing and accepting, even as they set limits.

Using harsh punishment can lead adults to believe that they are in control again, and it can help adults to feel better by discharging their anger. However, there are several problems with punishment.

Some of the problems associated with punishing the child due to an anger outburst include the following:

a. The child was already in pain before the problematic behavior occurred. Furthermore, it is this pain that has led to the acting out of anger. Punishment adds to this pain, adds to the child's anger, and can easily lead to more acting-out behavior. The pain should ideally be soothed instead of compounded.

b. Punishment does not teach children to do something they do not know how to do. Children who do not know how to cope with pain do not learn to cope with it by punishment.

c. Punishment teaches that the reason to behave in accordance with adult expectations is to avoid more punishment. We would ideally want children to behave in a certain way in order to take joy in contribution, rather than from fear of punishment.

d. Punishment models one person exercising power over another individual. Children will be more likely to copy this dynamic with their peers and siblings and to act it out in their play. Physical punishment is likely to lead the child to increased aggression.

e. Punishment can teach children that they are bad for acting as they did.

f. Punishment can lead to a focus on getting caught, and it may lead to more sneaky attempts to repeat similar behavior.

g. Although the undesired behavior often stops in the moment when an adult implements punishment, punishment does not make the behavior less likely to recur in the future.

h. Children tend to adapt to punishment, which leads the adult to use harsher punishments over time.

As you reflect on your own childhood, was there a time that you deserved to be punished? Did the punishment help you? Even if you believe it did help you, would there have been an even better way to help you? What did you really need at that time?

Even after children's behavioral expressions of anger, we may continue to set limits on such actions by telling children what we will not allow and why we have become concerned enough to restrict their actions. Such restrictions are imposed in order to protect the child or to protect others or the rights of others. This can be done using a caring tone of voice and without any shaming of the child or any intention to cause suffering. If the child expresses anger at the limit-setting, we can demonstrate an interest in the child's feelings and inquire about the unsatisfied needs. When a child has caused damages due to aggression, we can discuss a way to have the child make amends for the damages.

When we do set such limits or assign a consequence as part of the restorative process (soon to be described), we also want to remember that we are contributing to some needs at the expense of the child's need for autonomy (i.e., making one's own choices). Furthermore, we may incur some of the problems just described in relation to punishment. As a result, we will want to show sensitivity in setting the limit. In addition, we will ideally find other ways we can help contribute to the child's need for autonomy. This may include playing games with the child or doing activities in which the child can make choices.

17.

Empathize and Then Express

In an earlier chapter, guidelines were presented for empathizing with the child who is upset but has not acted out the anger. Even after an outburst, empathy is often needed. Once the child has calmed down enough so that everyone is safe, we can let the child know that we can now talk about what is bothering him or her. Waiting until the child has ended the outburst before giving our full attention reinforces the value of self-calming. We can then proceed to empathize with the child's feelings and needs. Having acted out anger, the child may experience additional sadness, guilt, shame, and fear of retaliation. We may ask children how they feel, after having expressed the anger as they did. We can use the same empathy skills already discussed to help the child to become aware of additional feelings and needs related to the behavioral expression of anger.

We have now listened to the child, helping to get his or her needs onto the table. An important step in working with a child on his or her challenging behavior is to get the adult's concerns into the open, as well. Before we do this, we want to wait until the child has calmed down and there is little chance of a re-escalation of emotions into volatile behavior. But how do we as adults express our own concerns to children?

Having calmed ourselves down (and having helped the child to calm down, through empathy), it is now reasonable to admit our own feelings related to the child's recent behavior. Once again, it is helpful to wait until the child is no longer in a triggered state. When children are more relaxed, they can be more attentive to our messages.

It is very helpful to keep an evenness to our emotions, if possible. The goal is not to instill fear in children but to show them that their behavioral choices have affected us. Doing this effectively involves speaking of our own feelings and the needs behind those feelings, not giving a lecture. Lectures are especially unhelpful during the midst of stress immediately following a behavioral incident.

When referring to a child's behavior using *NVC*, we seek to make an objective observation of what the child did. To describe our observations in an objective manner, we can describe the behavior as though a neutral person were witnessing the behavior, without any additional analysis of the behavior. We do not want to make a judgment of what the child did. Such judgments tend to lead to defensiveness.

Examples of objective observations include the following:
"You took the poster off the wall."
"You kicked your sister."
"You called Jimmy a jerk."

In contrast, judgments include the following:
"You went wild and acted like a crazy person."
"You disrespected your mother."
"You do whatever you want to do, no matter what I tell you."

To practice this step, observe a child and try to describe (in writing) the child's actions without any analysis or judgment. Simply describe what the child is doing.

By referencing the child's behavior, we can continue and state our feelings that are triggered by the behavior. We can also express the needs that are associated with these feelings. Very often, we will express needs for safety, consideration, and respect.

For example, we might tell Jennifer: "When you kicked over the trash can in class, I was very concerned. I want all the children to learn in a safe environment." (The teacher expresses her need for safety and the uneasy feeling she has when that need is not satisfied. This type of statement is preferable to telling the child that she "threw a fit" or acted "like a fool.")

After we have expressed our behavioral observations and our feelings and needs, we can ask the child to repeat back what we expressed. The idea is to determine if the message was understood.

To practice putting these steps together, think of an action taken by a child that may trigger your frustration. Try to describe the behavior using objective language that does not judge the behavior. Then describe your feelings that are triggered by the child's behavior, being careful not to blame the child for your feelings. Can you also state the need of yours that is unsatisfied by the child's behavior?

Can you also recall a time when you made a statement (out of anger) that sounded like a judgment? How might you have described your feelings that were underneath the anger? Was there sadness or fear?

We may also want to make a direct request of the child. We might simply say, for example, "Would you be willing to pick up the trash on the floor from the knocked-over can?" As discussed earlier, using a request rather than a demand will trigger less resistance. And the child has the opportunity to act out of concern for others, rather than fear of punishment.

Can you identify a request that you might want to make of a child, based on his or her action that triggered a strong feeling within you?

18.

Ask Thought-Provoking Questions

We have already expressed our feelings related to the child's behavioral expression of anger. Well after the child has calmed down, and there is little chance of a re-escalation of emotions into volatile behavior, we can ask the child questions to stimulate learning and personal growth.

As Costello, Wachtel, and Wachtel described in their book *Restorative Circles in Schools* (2010), the field of restorative practices provides a series of questions to help people to reflect on their past actions. Such questions include the following:

- What happened?

- What were you thinking of at the time?

- What have you thought about since?

- Who has been affected by what you have done?

- In what way have they been affected?

- What do you think you need to do to make things right?

© 2010 International Institute for Restorative Practices

We can nonjudgmentally ask what the child was thinking about at the time of the behavior episode. If we were to ask this question using a judgmental tone or a threatening voice, the child's response would often be to tell us what we want to hear. If children believe their responses will be the basis for punishment, then they may similarly tell us what we want to hear. This would defeat the purpose of helping to stimulate learning in the child. Similarly, if we had not established an emotional connection with the child, we could expect a similar type of "people-pleasing" response from him or her. Our goal is to foster rational thinking, so we want to encourage the child's honesty. In order to ask the question in the spirit it is intended, we may need to take the time to calm ourselves once again and to get into an open-minded, compassionate state.

Then we can ask what the child has been thinking about since the time of the incident. For example, we can be curious as to whether the child has been troubled about the past behavior. Alternatively, maybe the child has not thought about the events all that much. Again, we would want to ask these questions with a full acceptance of the child's possible responses.

We can also ask who has been affected, and in what way, by the child's behavior. Some children will have difficulty realizing the full scope of consequences that have occurred as a result of their past actions. If this is the case, we can follow up with questions asking about specific parties that may have been affected.

In addition, we can ask what can be done to repair damages. This question encourages self-responsibility and is solution-oriented rather than punitive.

If others have been harmed by the child's behavior, it can be helpful for the others to describe the impact that the incident has had on them. With the help of a trained facilitator, conferencing can be used to bring the involved parties together to discuss the behavior and its impact. This process is described in greater detail in the above-mentioned book about restorative circles.

It may also be worth asking one or more of the following: How do you feel about yourself after what happened? How would you like to handle this situation if it happened again? What can you do to ensure that you handle things in this way? How do you think you would feel about yourself if you handled things in the way you would have liked? We want to avoid overwhelming the child with questions, so it may realistically be possible to ask only some of these questions in one session.

Let's take an example of a boy who, during an anger display a day earlier, ran his arm across the teacher's desk. His action caused all the desk items to go flying and a glass picture frame to crack. By being asked the above restorative questions, the boy may indicate that (when he did what he did) he was thinking about the teacher's calling on everyone else but him. Since then, however, he was thinking about the damaged picture frame and feeling sad about that. He may report that he was sad that the teacher might be upset about the broken item. He might say that, to make things right, he needs to pay back the teacher for the broken frame.

Having addressed the specific incident that occurred, we can still do more to help the child learn how to avoid such behavioral episodes in the future. We can extend an invitation to the child to come up with possible solutions that will address the needs of both the child and the adult, should the child again be overcome with strong emotions.

An important step is to demonstrate an understanding of the child's needs at the time of the behavioral episode. We then want to remind the child of our needs that were not satisfied by the child's behavior. Finally, we want to ask the child to help us figure out how everyone's needs can be satisfied in the future. This process has the advantage of helping the child to develop problem-solving skills.

For example, we might say the following to Jennifer, who kicked the trash can: "I know how angry you were and how important respect is to you. And now you understand how important safety is to me. I'd like us to come up with a way to meet both of our needs. Do you have any ideas?"

We can also ask thought-provoking questions to ourselves, if the child is not capable of answering such questions. We can ask the following questions: What can we do to prevent similar problems in the future? What was the sequence of events that occurred before the outburst? Can we teach the child any additional skills to deal with his or her feelings?

Part V

Closing

In this guide, I have described a model for preventing anger, dealing with anger before behavioral escalation, and responding after a child's behavioral episode.

I have described use of a variety of strategies. When used properly, these are valuable means of preventing and de-escalating anger while promoting self-responsibility. When we find ourselves unsure of what we are trying to accomplish when dealing with an angry child, we can stop and ask ourselves if we are engaging in one of these actions. If we are doing something else, then we need to be sure we are not escalating the situation.

The interventions in this model can be summarized by the acronym RESPECT. The RESPECT approach includes the following strategies:

R: Requests
E: Empathy (for oneself and others)

S: Self-expression (and Stress management)
P: Problem-solving (and Pleasurable activities)
E: Encouragement (of contribution)
C: Calming (and Caring limits)
T: Thought-provoking questions

Even with the best of intentions, however, we adults will sometimes act without full consciousness. We will sometimes lack the patience to listen to the child. We will sometimes lose our cool. We will occasionally resort to our old ways of reacting. By being gentle with ourselves, we can allow awareness of the discrepancy between our actions and our ideals. In these instances, there is potential for enormous opportunity. We can let the child know that we are still learning. We can tell the child that we tried our best, but we acted differently than we would like to act in the future. We can show any sadness we may have about our recent actions. By showing the child that we do not need to punish ourselves for our actions, we set an effective example of humility. The child then sees the possibility of learning from behavior without self-punishment.

19.

Comprehension Check

Here are several important points described within this guide.

- Using Marshall Rosenberg's *Nonviolent Communication* (*NVC*), we can view everything people do as an attempt to meet a need. Common needs that children are trying to meet through their challenging behaviors are autonomy, fun, stimulation, and respect.
- An important skill for adults and children to learn before an intense anger episode is self-calming. Toward this aim, one technique that can be used is the calming breath.
- A valuable tool for calming ourselves when we are upset is the process of self-empathy. This process, which includes paying attention to both our feelings and needs, can help us to act in accordance with our values when we are triggered by a child's challenging behavior. We can begin to learn how to provide self-empathy before we are overcome with strong emotions. When we notice that we are negatively judging a child, we can seek to identify our unsatisfied needs.
- *NVC* maintains that feelings may be triggered by others but are not caused by them.
- A powerful way to teach children to give respect is to model it for them.

- By seeking cooperation, rather than compliance, we show respect and help to satisfy the child's need for autonomy. We can often make requests, rather than demands, in order to encourage children to act out of a desire to contribute. When we must make demands, we are better off doing it with care and sensitivity to the child's feelings.

- We can reduce the chances of anger displays by engaging in occasional, pleasurable activities with children; by encouraging contribution; by lowering unrealistic, stressful demands on them; and by preparing them for stress that cannot be lowered.

- A basic need of humans is to contribute to others. We can encourage the child's contribution if we report the feelings that are stimulated within us and the needs of ours that are satisfied by the child's gesture. We can even encourage the child's efforts to express frustration and anger, when such efforts are done in ways that help to satisfy our needs. We can view such expressions by children as a form of contribution.

- When it comes to expressing their anger in better ways, sometimes we must either break the task into smaller steps or prompt the behavior that we would like children to display. Eventually, children will not need such prompting.

- With the help of problem-solving techniques, children can learn to consider potential consequences of their actions.

- Empathy with children who are upset involves taking the time to help them to identify their feelings and the underlying needs behind those feelings. We usually get better results by empathizing first, before attempting to problem-solve with children.

- We can set caring limits to protect people and their rights and property.

- When we are triggered by children's recent actions, we are not in a good place to provide empathy. At such times, we may find it helpful to give ourselves self-empathy.
- Punishment teaches children to comply in order to avoid further punishment. We would ideally want children to behave in a certain way in order to take joy in contribution. We would not want them to act primarily from fear of punishment.
- After we empathize with the child, we can express our own feelings and needs related to the child's behavioral incident. When referring to a child's behavior (after emotions have cooled down), we can strive to make an objective observation of what the child did.
- Well after we have expressed feelings about the behavioral incident, we can ask the child thought-provoking questions about it. For example, we can ask what he or she was thinking about at the time of the behavior. We need to be in a compassionate state of mind to do this effectively.
- If others have been harmed by the child's behavior, it can be helpful for the others to describe the impact that the incident has had on them.
- We can also invite children to discuss with us how they can act in the future to simultaneously meet their needs as well as our own. This process helps to stimulate their thinking brains.
- We are better off attempting to de-escalate, rather than escalate, anger. We can stop and ask ourselves if we are engaging in empathy, self-empathy, self-calming, self-expression, problem-solving, or setting limits with care. If we are doing something else in our interactions with an angry child, then we need to be sure we are not escalating the situation.
- Despite our best intentions, we adults will sometimes

accidentally return to old patterns of behavior. By being gentle with ourselves, we can approach the child with sadness about our less-than-helpful actions but without need for self-punishment. By showing children that we are still learning, we help them learn compassion for themselves.

20.

Examples

In each of the following examples, the helping adult uses strategies described throughout this guide to prevent anger, de-escalate anger, or respond to challenging behavioral episodes. These examples illustrate possible statements that could be made by helping adults. Try to remember that there are many other statements that a helping adult can make.

Example #1: This first example takes place at a school. A six-year-old boy has addressed his teacher several times that morning in a way that she did not like.

(The teacher noticed herself starting to raise her voice at the child. She then checked in with her feelings. She noticed herself feeling angry and recalled her strategy of taking calming breaths when she was becoming angry. With a classroom of children, she had time for only one slow, calm breath. She then checked in with her needs. She noticed that her need for respect was not met. She noticed herself feeling sadness underneath the anger, and she took another calming breath. Without the time to have a conversation with the child, the teacher sent him to the main office to speak with the school counselor.

Now in the counselor's office, the child sits quietly, saying nothing and looking nervous.)

Counselor: I heard something happened in class today. (The counselor gently eases into conversation so as to create an environment in which the child is not on the defense. This is also an effort to show respect to the child.)

(The child still says nothing. From past experience with adults, the child is afraid of getting scolded.)

Counselor: Are you afraid to tell me? Maybe you think that I will yell at you? (The counselor takes a guess concerning the child's feelings, in order to foster connection with the child.)

(The child shrugs his shoulders. He is still reluctant.)

Counselor: I am concerned about you and the others in the classroom. I want to make sure that everyone is treated with respect. (The counselor tries to reassure the child. The counselor is also expressing her need, and presumably the teacher's, for respect.)

(The child begins to show an openness in body language.)

Counselor: I heard that you said to your teacher, "You're stupid." Is that what happened? (The counselor uses a direct quote, rather than evaluating the child's behavior. A direct quote is an example of a neutral observation. Wanting to establish a partnership with the child, the counselor refrains from an accusatory, hostile tone.)

Child: She took my game.

Counselor: Oh, I see. Did you feel angry? (The counselor is trying to get to the feeling.)

(The child nods his head to indicate agreement.)

Counselor: You really like having that game to play when YOU want to, don't you? (The counselor is attempting to establish partnership.) Why do you think she took the game? (The counselor tries to foster an understanding of the rules.)

Child: You can't bring games to school.

Counselor: It sounds like you know the rule, don't you? You decided to bring the game to school, even though you know the rule? (The counselor shows nonjudgmental curiosity about the child's choice. This is also an example of a thought-provoking question.)

(The child nods in agreement.)

Counselor: It was very important to you to bring the game to school, wasn't it? (The counselor is still creating partnership in hopes of understanding the child's underlying need.)

Child: Jamal said he'd be my friend if I let him play.

Counselor: Oh, so you really wanted Jamal to be your friend? I can understand why you brought in the game. (The counselor is empathizing further, taking a guess as to the child's underlying need. Friendship or companionship is a need that we all have.)

Child: He's nice to me.

Counselor: So you wanted a friend, and you were willing to break the rule and even have your game taken away so you could have a friend? (The counselor is asking another thought-provoking question to stimulate the child's thinking skills.)

(The child nods in agreement.)

Counselor: Was there any other way you could be friends with Jamal without breaking the rule? (The counselor is using problem-solving to build thinking skills.)

Child: I could have played the game with him after school.

Counselor: That sounds like a good idea. What do you think would have happened if you played it with him after school instead? (Inquiring about possible consequences is a part of the problem-solving process.)

(As the dialogue continues, the child is learning that an adult can be a helpful resource, rather than a punishing figure. At a later point, once the child's feelings have been fully acknowledged, the counselor also speaks with the child about the way the child expressed his anger. The counselor helps the child understand how the teacher might have felt. The counselor eventually encourages the child to apologize to the teacher. An effort is made to avoid punishment to the extent that this does not conflict with school policy. The counselor also teaches the words to express anger. In days to come, when the teacher catches the child using these feeling words, the teacher can express appreciation for the respect she experiences. The teacher may say something like the following: "When you use your feeling words to tell me how you feel, I am so pleased by the respect you show." This acknowledgment of the child's contribution (to the teacher's need for respect) functions as a type of positive reinforcement or encouragement for the child's use of feeling words.)

Example #2: In this example, a parent (P) interacts with a child (C) who does not want to do her chore of cleaning her bedroom.

P: I notice you haven't cleaned your room. (The parent makes a behavioral observation, free of judgment, in order to convey respect.)

C: I don't want to.

P: You don't feel like cleaning your room right now. Maybe you just want to relax now? (The parent takes a guess as to the need of the child. Relaxation is a need that we all have.)

C: Yeah. I just want to play my game right now. I'll do it later.

P: You want to play your game now. Maybe you want to have some fun before you start doing something that isn't fun for you? (This is an attempt to empathize with the child. Fun is also a need that we all have.)

C: Yeah. Can I just do it after dinner?

P: I guess that's okay. (The parent reflects on her feelings. She is a little irritated. She asks herself what her needs are. She notices that she has a need for cooperation. She reflects on the child's request and decides that her needs, and the child's, can be satisfied after dinner. The parent feels comfortable with the agreement, even though it was not her initial plan.)

(After dinner, the child is still postponing the chore. The parent begins to approach the child to reprimand her but quickly catches herself. She is not rushed and has the time to take five calming breaths before approaching her. While breathing slowly, the parent asks herself how she is feeling.

She easily notices anger. As a result, she asks herself what judgment she is making. She realizes that she is judging the child for being lazy and spoiled. She knows that her judgments reflect an unsatisfied need of hers. She asks herself if there is another feeling underneath the anger. She notices worry. She asks herself what needs of hers are not satisfied at this moment. She notices a need for safety, as she recalls her child's sleepwalking issue. She feels a tear going down her face. Instead of wanting to reprimand her child, this parent now wants to embrace her child and keep her safe. The parent then returns to the interaction.)

P: Remember we agreed that you would clean your room after dinner?

C: Yeah, but I'm tired now. Can I do it tomorrow?

P: I hear that you still don't want to clean your room now. It's important to me that I can trust you will do what you promised. It's also important to me that your room is a safe place to be in, so you don't trip over all those toys and games. Would you be willing to work on cleaning for 20 minutes now and then finish tomorrow? (The parent begins to express her own needs, including trust and safety. She follows with a direct request, rather than choosing to command the child.)

C: I want to do it all tomorrow. I will have more energy then.

(The parent becomes aware of frustration and needs for respect and trust. She takes a calming breath to help her speak.)

P: I'm frustrated that we made an agreement, and you are going back on it. I really value trust in our relationship. I also know that you're tired now. And you expect to have more energy tomorrow to clean your room. Maybe there's a way we can both be satisfied. (The parent uses self-expression, talking about her own feelings and needs.)

C: How about I put away the toys and games in front of my bed now and do the closet tomorrow?

P: Okay. That works for me. I will check your progress in 10 minutes.

(The child follows through as discussed, leaving the needs of both parent and child satisfied. There are also many other ways that both parties could have their needs satisfied.)

Example #3: In this example, the school disciplinarian (D) speaks with Johnny (J), who walked out of the classroom without permission.

D: So I hear that you left the classroom. Is that what happened? (In order to show respect, the adult is trying to establish the facts without evaluating them.)

J: I don't have to do anything I don't want to do. (The child is visibly angry and is asserting his autonomy.)

D: You really didn't want to be in that class, did you? (Sidestepping the child's defensive statement, the adult is establishing rapport and empathy. The adult has learned of the child's need for autonomy. But she believes there is another need that has not yet been identified.)

J: I hate school.

D: Something about school is really bothering you. (The adult is relating to the child and avoiding a lecture at this moment. There is then silence for about a minute.)

J: Everyone laughs when I read out loud. (The child's anger turns to sadness.)

D: You don't like it when people laugh at you. Does it bother you because you want people to be considerate of you? (The disciplinarian guesses if an underlying need of Johnny's is consideration.)

J: What does that mean?

D: It means when people care about how you are feeling.

J: I want them to think I'm smart.

D: Oh, okay. You would like respect, too, wouldn't you? (The adult points to the possible underlying psychological need.)

J: Yeah. How do I get good at reading?

(As the conversation continues, the student develops motivation to become a better reader. School interventions could also be planned to help Johnny develop reading skills. Because Johnny has a history of difficulties with anger, the disciplinarian considers how demands on him might be lowered. Perhaps the teacher can refrain from requiring Johnny to read aloud at this point. Although Johnny had walked out of the classroom, the school policy does not require punishment. The disciplinarian avoids punishing but works with Johnny to apologize to the teacher for the exit. The following exchange occurs later in the conversation.)

D: So if you stay in the classroom, even though you don't like reading out loud, what do you think might happen to your reading? (The adult teaches a problem-solving skill of anticipating consequences.)

J: I would be a better reader?

D: Yes, you might learn to become a better reader. How does that sound?

J: Maybe my mom can practice reading at home with me. (The child offers his own strategy.)

(The conversation has shifted to the student's coming up with his own strategies to develop reading skills, and the problem-solving partnership has been strengthened.)

Example #4: In this example, Erica (E) is the daughter of divorced parents. She does not want to visit her father over the weekend. She tells her mother (M) that she is not going.

M: So you really don't want to visit Daddy this weekend.

E: I'm not going. He doesn't play with me. It's boring. He's too busy with his girlfriend.

M: You really want to have fun when you go there. And sometimes it isn't much fun for you. (The mother identifies an underlying need of fun.)

E: I don't like it. I'm not going anymore. (Erica starts to cry.)

M: You really don't want to go. You want to be able to make your own choices, don't you? (The mother detects an underlying need of choice or autonomy in her child. Several minutes later, Erica is more relaxed and is ready for problem-solving.)

M: Daddy really wants to see you. Do you have any ideas for how to handle this?

E: I can tell him I'm not coming over.

M: What if you also tell him how you feel when you visit? Maybe he would be willing to do something fun with you when you are there.

E: Maybe he will play with me if he knows how sad I get. Or maybe he will buy me a game I can play there by myself.

(With the child now in problem-solving mode, the interaction has progressed significantly.)

———————————

Example #5: At a summer overnight camp for children with behavioral challenges, Jason (J) sets fire to a backpack owned by his peer, Eddie (E). A shirt, a pair of shorts, and some playing cards are destroyed. The camp director (D) meets with the two boys the next morning after a cooling-down period to talk about what happened. Of course this is a serious incident, and there will be more to discuss later with the parents.

D: From what I was told, Jason, you set fire to Eddie's backpack. Is this what happened?

J: Yeah, but he was hitting me all day before that.

D: You were really angry, weren't you? Were you trying to get back at him? (Mutuality or fairness is a common need behind children's behavior.)

J: Yes! He shouldn't have messed with me.

D: Was it a matter of respect? (The camp director identifies another possible underlying need for Jason to confirm or deny.)

J: I don't want to look like a chump. (He nods in agreement.)

D: You must have been very upset, Jason, to start a fire. What happened is very serious though. Starting a fire is dangerous. People could have been badly hurt. Eddie, do you want to tell Jason how you are feeling?

E: My parents will be mad. They will want to sue. He ruined my stuff.

D: Are you mad yourself?

E: Yes. Wouldn't you be?

D: Are you also sad because the things that were burned mean something to you? (The camp director guesses at a possible feeling underneath the anger.)

E: Yes, but there is something even more important. I just don't like being disrespected like that.

D: I see. Respect is important to you as well, just like it is to Jason. Jason, how do you feel hearing this?

J: Sad. I'm sorry, Eddie.

D: Eddie, do you think there is anything that Jason can do to make things better between you both? (This is an example of a thought-provoking question. Other questions could also be used in this situation.)

E: He can pay for my stuff.

D: Jason, how does that sound to you? What do you think needs to be done to make things right? (This is another example of a thought-provoking question.)

J: Okay. I guess I owe him that much.

E: It's probably about $50.

D: Jason, I will need to let your parents know what happened when they arrive later today. They already know there was a serious incident at camp. If they agree with the plan, you and they can discuss how to pay for the damages. (This consequence is one of restorative justice, rather than an attempt to cause suffering. Throughout this process, the camp director has stayed connected with Jason.)

(Jason nods in agreement.)

D: We also need to talk about the hitting that was going on earlier. Eddie, were you mad at Jason about something? (The camp director recognizes that there are two perspectives in a conflict and that both sides have responsibility for their own actions.)

E: He just annoys me sometimes, so I hit him a few times.

D: What kinds of things does he do to annoy you?

E: He is always hanging on me, getting in my business. I don't like people knowing what I'm doing every second.

D: So you want your own space? I see. (An underlying need for space is identified.)

(Eddie nods in agreement.)

D: Is hitting him a good way of getting space? (This is a problem-solving question.)

E: I could have told him that I want him to stay away.

D: That might work better. Jason, do you need something more from Eddie so you can feel better?

J: I want him to keep his hands off me. And I want him to respect me.

E: Sorry for hitting you, Jason. I didn't mean to hurt you that much.

J: Okay.

D: Jason, I am still very concerned about the fire. This is a very serious matter that will have to be discussed further, including whether you can continue to remain at camp. If you are to remain at camp, I want you to be able to have fun here. But I need for everyone to be safe and for people's property to be safe. If you are to stay at this camp, how can you help me to trust that you will never do anything like this again?

J: I won't do it again. You can take those matches I found. (Jason is crying now.)

D: And I want you to meet with your counselor each evening to tell him how the day was for you. If anything is bothering you, I want you to tell him. And Eddie, I want all campers to keep their hands to themselves. No hitting. Understand?

(The counselor will also be guided to encourage Jason by expressing appreciation to Jason each time that Jason expresses his feelings calmly, rather than acting out aggressively. The camp director still has to discuss the situation further with the parents of both parties. But the two children might both be able to stay at camp for the rest of the summer.)

Example #6: Rhonda (R) is sent to see the school counselor (C) after several incidents of getting out of her designated place in the back of the line to move to the front.

C: Can you tell me what happened?

R: It's not fair. Why do I always have to be at the end of the line?

C: You don't like to have to always stand in the back of the line, do you? (The counselor shows acceptance of the child's feelings.)

R: I want to be near Ava. She's my cousin.

C: Okay, you like being near Ava. (The counselor encourages Rhonda's verbal expression.)

R: She protects me when they pick on me. (The child identifies her own need for safety.)

C: Other children are picking on you?

R: Two of the boys hit me when no one was looking.

C: You don't like getting hit. I don't blame you. Can you think of any other things to do so you don't get in trouble and you don't get hit? (The counselor moves into a problem-solving process.)

R: I can tell the teacher that they're hitting me. But I don't want to be a snitch. People don't like snitches.

C: You really want to handle things without telling, don't you? Maybe you want the others to accept you? (The counselor validates the child's need, which has to do with a connection with others.)

R: Yeah. But I could help them with their work in class, and maybe they will like me better.

(The student comes up with a new strategy on her own to end the hitting without the need to violate her values or the class rules. Although the strategy may not work, the problem-solving process has begun. If problems persist, perhaps demands could be lowered by the teacher's working with the class on how to line up in an orderly manner. As a result, there could be fewer incidents as the children are in line.)

Example #7: Eight-year-old Damien (D) has been frustrated with his brother, who has been using his toys without permission. Damien has had an anger episode in which he threw books and toys across his bedroom, cursed at his mother (M), and banged his head against the wall. His mother witnessed the episode. She was very upset by what she saw.

(Damien's mother was quickly aware of her need for safety and her need for effectiveness, as a parent. She knew she had to set limits to protect Damien and herself from injury. She also knew she wanted to maintain a connection during limit-setting. To do this, she reminded herself that her son was very upset in order to do what he did. She would plan to find out more about his feelings. She approached Damien slowly to let him know she wanted to help. When it seemed safe, she held him to stop him from banging his head. She also took five calming breaths so she could speak calmly. She then checked in with herself to find out what she was feeling. She noticed she was angry about the cursing. She asked herself what her need was, beneath the judgment of her anger. She discovered that she had a need for respect. She was appalled by the lack of respect in the words used by her son. She took a few more calming breaths and reflected on the value of her need for respect. She began to soften up as she saw how important respect was for her. Her anger turned to sadness. As she became sad and less angry, she did not feel the desire to make her son suffer from unnecessary punishment. But she knew that she would later like him to take responsibility for the damages he caused by destroying his books and toys.

She turned her attention to Damien to empathize with him. She asked him if he was extremely angry when he did what he did. He told her that he was. He also revealed that he hated it when his brother took his toys. She asked him if he needed respect and consideration. He said he definitely did. Once Damien's needs were revealed, his mother expressed her own sadness about his management of his feelings.)

M: When you threw your books and called me a jerk, I was very sad. I really want respect and consideration, just like you do. And when you hit your head, I was scared that you would get very hurt. I want you to be safe. (Respect, consideration, and safety are all needs.) Are you willing to express your anger using words and a calm body before taking further action? (Damien's mother is making a request.)

D: Yes, Mommy. (Damien appears remorseful.)

(The next day, his mother asks Damien who was affected by what he had done and what he could do to make things right. Damien acknowledges that his mother was sad and scared. He proposes a plan to pay for the damages out of his allowance. Damien is sad but accepts the responsibility. His mother acknowledges her own sadness as well.

His mother also embarks on a plan of expressing encouragement each time Damien tells her his feelings of frustration or anger. At first, she has to ask him to name his feelings so that she has a chance to provide immediate encouragement. Over time, after Damien is consistently reporting his feelings appropriately, his mother will discontinue her prompting of his feelings and expect him to approach her independently with his feelings of anger. She will continue to encourage his self-expression by showing appreciation for his management of anger.)

21.

Your Turn to Practice

In order to change from your usual way of responding to a new and more effective way, it is important to practice. Below I present some examples of what a child might say during a state of anger, so you can stop and reflect on a new response. Before creating your response, remember to consider what the child may feel and need as well as what you feel and need. I present a few possible answers on the next page. There are no wrong answers to what you may feel or need. In addition, you may think of responses that I did not consider.

a. In school, a girl walks out of class, yelling profanity about the school and teacher. What do you, as the teacher, feel and need? What does the child feel and need? What would you say?

b. At home, a child tells you (the parent) how much he hates the children on the block. He is sobbing as he speaks. What do you feel and need? What does the child feel and need? What would you say?

c. A child tells you that he hates how you act. (You can think of any action that you sometimes perform. You might even want to change this behavior. If you cannot think of one, you can use the example of making promises and not following through on them.) What do you feel and need? What does the child feel and need? What would you say?

a. I might be feeling any of a number of feelings such as angry, annoyed, frustrated, sad, or scared. I might need consideration, respect, cooperation, effectiveness, or order. By order, I mean that I want the classroom to run smoothly. By effectiveness, I mean that I want to be effective as a classroom teacher. The child might be feeling angry, enraged, frustrated, or afraid. Maybe she is having difficulty with the schoolwork or with a person in the classroom. Without more context, it is difficult to know what the child might need. I can imagine needs such as clarity, acceptance, respect, belonging, autonomy, and freedom. After a few deep breaths or another self-calming step, I might say to the child, "Something is really upsetting you, isn't it? Would you be willing to tell me about it?"

b. I might be feeling curious, sad, or confused. I might need connection, support, or contribution. In other words, I might get in touch with a strong need to support the child or contribute to his well-being. The child might be feeling sad, angry, ashamed, or depressed. Perhaps the child had a conflict with more than one of the children. The child might need companionship, belonging, or acceptance. I might say to the child, "Are you sad because you want a friend?"

c. Possible answers will vary based on the scenario. With the example of not following through on promises, I might be feeling guilty. I might have an unsatisfied need for integrity. If I feel especially guilty, then I am making a judgment about myself. I may then choose to also remind myself of what need contributed to my behavior. The child might feel angry as well as sad and disappointed. He may need trust or integrity. I might say to the child, "Are you angry because trust is important to you?"

22.

Final Thoughts

In this guide, I have presented a variety of action steps that can minimize children's anger, as well as other steps that can prevent a behavioral escalation once anger has emerged. I have also described what to do in the event of a behavioral expression of anger.

Several *NVC* strategies have included empathizing with the child, empathizing with our own adult feelings and needs, expressing ourselves respectfully to the child, and balancing each of these in our interactions with the child. Other strategies have included calming rituals, stress management, pleasurable activities, caring limits, thought-provoking questions, and problem-solving. I have also described how to encourage children to express anger using feeling words. Respect has been a core theme throughout this guide, and the strategies reflect this important human need. This emphasis on a mutual respect is in spite of a traditional emphasis on a power-over approach, in which the adult is in power and the child's job is to comply.

As children observe our efforts to help them, they receive a powerful example of how to help themselves as well as interact cooperatively with others. They may benefit as well from direct instruction of these communication skills, particularly in expressing themselves to others, listening to others, and making requests. As we develop these skills ourselves, we will become more proficient in teaching them to children during moments of calmness. As we gain confidence in our own understanding and knowledge of anger, we will be able to teach children about what anger means, how needs contribute to feelings, and how thoughts can lead to anger. This learning will gradually help to prevent children's anger from turning into behavioral episodes.

I encourage readers to reflect upon these strategies and to discuss them with others. I also encourage readers who are frustrated by their own approaches to attempt these strategies and to evaluate the effects. It may not be easy to use this approach, especially the language of empathy, but this may be an opportunity for much-needed change. I also want to remind readers that a great deal of benefit may come from welcoming the child's feelings and needs, even if we cannot come up with the words to label these feelings and needs.

In closing, I wish you the best of luck in your efforts to relate positively to children, even when they are angry.

References

Baumrind, D. (1967). Child care practices anteceding three patterns of preschool behavior. *Genetic Psychology Monographs, 75,* 43-88.

Costello, B., Wachtel, J., & Wachtel, T. (2010). *Restorative circles in schools: Building community and enhancing learning.* Bethlehem, PA: International Institute for Restorative Practices.

Greene, R. (2014). *The explosive child: A new approach for understanding and parenting easily frustrated, chronically inflexible children* (rev. ed.). New York, NY: HarperCollins.

Hart, S., & Kindle Hodson, V. (2006). *Respectful parents, respectful kids: 7 keys to turn family conflict into co-operation.* Encinitas, CA: PuddleDancer Press.

Ragsdale, S., & Saylor, A. (2007). *Great group games: 175 boredom-busting, zero-prep team builders for all ages.* Minneapolis, MN: Search Institute Press.

Rosenberg, M. (2003). *Nonviolent communication: A language of life* (2nd ed.). Encinitas, CA: PuddleDancer Press.

Shure, M. (1992). *I can problem solve: An interpersonal cognitive problem-solving program for children.* Champaign, IL: Research Press.

Recommended Reading

The following works are recommended in addition to each of the previously noted references.

Cohen, L. (2002). *Playful parenting.* New York, NY: Ballantine.

Dreikurs, R., & Cassel, P. (1990). *Discipline without tears* (2nd ed.). New York, NY: EP Dutton.

Faber, A., & Mazlish, E. (1980). *How to talk so kids will listen & listen so kids will talk.* New York, NY: Avon.

Goleman, D. (1995). *Emotional intelligence: Why it can matter more than IQ.* New York, NY: Bantam.

Gottman, J., & DeClaire, J. (1997). *The heart of parenting: Raising an emotionally intelligent child.* New York, NY: Simon & Schuster.

Kashtan, I. (2004). *Parenting from your heart: Sharing the gifts of compassion, connection, and choice.* Encinitas, CA: PuddleDancer Press.

Kohn, A. (2005). *Unconditional parenting: Moving from rewards and punishments to love and reason.* New York, NY: Atria.

Markham, L. (2012). *Peaceful parents, happy kids: How to stop yelling and start connecting.* New York, NY: Penguin Group.

Siegel, D., & Hartzell, M. (2004). *Parenting from the inside out.* New York, NY: Tarcher.